"As I'm owned by a fellow hairy equine I can relate to m[...] love of food and his quite often boredom at having to rid[...] herself, if she were so inclined. I love Fridays, as Hovis's [...] his one liners have me in stitches. I for one cannot watch [...]

I think anyone, even none horse enthusiasts would enjoy [...] and humour and I think selling his works in aid of equines I [...] [...]mous."
Tess Pugh

"Humorous side to horsemanship"
Nicola Latham

"Hovis' diary is exactly what I think my horse would write if I left a laptop lying around"
Gemma Teed

"I work full time but on Fridays we get to finish at 1 pm. I check the HH forum every ten minutes or so from about 1030am onwards hoping to read Hovis's diary before I leave. If I go home disappointed because Hovis slept in and didnt get on the laptop in time, then first thing monday morning before I do ·any work, I search for it. Once read, I'm happy and can start work!

I think Hovis's diary is very funny and I actually believe it all to have happened, just like I believe everything on Emmerdale to be happening for real too.

Cant wait for the publication!!! I shall be ordering several copies, one for myself and a few more to give to my "horsey friends with a sense of humour" who I know will enjoy the read.
All for a great cause too!

Keep up the good work Hovis"
Karen Benbow

"Hovis Friday Diary – straight from the horses mouth, girth busting laughs"
Kim Preskey

"As a regular reader of Hovis' exploits from the very beginning, I have been hoping he would manage to get himself a publishing deal and this is great news, we get to catch up with the action and a great cause will raise lots of money. Three cheers for Hovis, now lets hear no more of the infamous 'Casa del pero'"
Sandra

"Hovis is the best thing since sliced bread"
Candy Wood

"Hovis "the Destroyer" is a legend"
Debbie Young

In loving memory of
Minnie "Moo" Marshall
and all the other horses we've loved and lost.
May we all meet again someday over the Rainbow Bridge

HOVIS'
Friday Diary
From The Beginning
—— 2008 — 2010 ——
Karen Thompson

Photo: Simon Orr

Published by Bransby Horses
Registered charity number 1075601
Bransby Horses, Bransby, Lincoln, LN1 2PH
www.bransbyhorses.co.uk

First published in Great Britain by Bransby Horses 2011

Pictures by Pilar Larcade

Any views or opinions presented are solely those of the author and do not necessarily
represent the views of Bransby Horses

Produced in Great Britain by In Sync Design

A CIP catalogue record for this book is available from the British Library

Paperback ISBN: 978-0-9568604-0-8

Acknowledgements

There are many people without whom this book would not have been possible and mentioning them all would fill a book in its own right. You all know who you are but there a special few that deserve a specific mention:

Firstly the community of the Horse and Hound online forum - without your enthusiasm, motivation and goodwill this book wouldn't have happened at all. Thank you for your continued support.

Pilar Larcade, without who I wouldn't have the amazing drawings in this book, that so bring to life Hovis' exploits. Pilar donated her time and talent to this project for free and for that I will always be in her debt. Born in Argentina but raised in the UK Pilar is an exceptional artist whose love of horses started at a young age inspired by the race horses she saw whilst visiting friends in Newmarket. If you ask Pilar's mother when she knew her daughter was going to be an artist she will cite the example of a young Pilar drawing dapples all over the arm of the sofa she liked to practise her "riding" on to make it more "life like"!

Details for contacting Pilar and looking at her incredible work can be found on her website http://pilar-larcade.110mb.com or on Facebook where she is found as Pilar Larcade, Artist.

Jo Snell and Verity Chappell from Bransby Horses, for their tireless enthusiasm, dedication and utter faith in Hovis and I (!!).

Carole Bacon and Sandra Greener from Bransby Horses, for their hawk eyed proof reading of my (or Hovis'?!) awful spelling.

Adele Crowther from In Sync Design for her enthusiasm, expertise and endless patience.

Simon Orr for the several hours spent stalking Hovis around the field with a camera (and for the green slobber down his very white sleeves that may never wash out...)

My husband, Brian, for all his help and encouragement. From the work he did with Hovis as a baby, to the endless driving me about in the lorry, to the short notice stand ins at the shows where I was too scared to warm up! Thank you babe for turning Hovis into the horse he is. Love you always.

My family and friends, for their understanding that Fridays aren't Fridays until I've written Hovis' Diary. Thank you for your love, support and occasional kick up the bottom. I love you all!

Finally, and most importantly, the man himself, my beautiful boy, Hovis. Some of us never get to meet our horse of a lifetime and I remind myself every day what a star I have the pleasure of owning.

I couldn't write this Diary if I didn't have the most loving, comical, frustrating and intelligent horse I could ever wish for. Searching for things to write about is never an issue, in fact sometime I have to tone it down for fear no one would believe me! He is a character who brightens the life of everyone he meets and moreover he makes me smile every single day.

I love you big man, more than you'll ever know.

A word from the Author

I never set out to write a book, although I've always wanted to.

At school I loved English with a passion and thanks to some amazing English teachers it turned out to be a subject I found effortless and enjoyable. However, heeding my father's advice to do what he classed as a "meaningful degree", I ended up falling back on my other love – science – and did a degree in Biochemistry at Birmingham University.

But I never ever lost my love of English – as a peek at my groaning bookcase will testify – and I have always harboured an incredible passion to write.

In the October of 2008, nearly a year to the day that I bought my beloved Clydesdale Hovis, I was on the Horse and Hound online forum and noted how much unhappiness there was; people losing horses, horses being injured or being diagnosed as critically ill. So on a whim I wrote a very short spoof "Diary" entry written by Hovis himself in an attempt to lift the mood. To my amazement I was inundated with messages of support and thanks and the following week was plagued by demands for his next "entry".

Hovis' Friday Diary was born.

Now over two years later Hovis' Friday Diary has become something of an institution with an army of followers and a weekly entry that has been known to provoke quite a demanding response if not published by lunchtime on Friday!! As time has gone on, and due in no small part to huge encouragement from members of the Horse and Hound online forum, I began to toy with the idea of publishing them. The only stumbling point for me was the fact I'd never written the Diary entries to make money; I write because I enjoy writing and it gives me huge pleasure to know others enjoy my work. With this in mind I started to ponder donating the profit to charity....

So why Bransby Horses?

The answer is simple and two fold.

Firstly I live in Lincolnshire so they are my "home" large equine charity. Known as the silent giant amongst their peers and other organisations, Bransby is probably one of the least publically known of the large equine charities. Their tireless work with the RSPCA, BHS and other welfare organisations to provide a safe haven for abused and abandoned animals is truly amazing. The facilities they provide are top notch and this combined with a very real and practical focus on education, training and prevention of cruelty really strikes a cord with me.

Secondly I chose Bransby as there is a wonderful link between the birth place of Hovis' Friday Diary and the charity:
In September 2009 a late night post on the Horse and Hound online forums from a member of the public concerned about two malnourished elderly horses sparked a reaction, that those using the forums are possibly used to, but to the outside world was nothing short of amazing. From raising awareness of the horses plight at Burghley Horse Trials (tragically only a few short miles from where the animals were located) to organising on site meetings with welfare organisations, within hours the might of the HHO community was focussed on saving these two horses. Nicknamed Carrot and Spud by their rescuers, the duo now reside at Bransby Horses where they will see out their days in comfort and happiness.

So to close the circle all the profit from this book will be put into a trust for Carrot and Spud to ensure that no matter what the future entails for them they will continue to receive the highest levels of care and attention they could possibly hope for.
Without the Horse and Hound online forum Hovis' Friday Diary would not exist and without the forum these two beautiful animals would possibly not be here today.

Sometimes I think life has a funny way of falling into place doesn't it?

BRANSBY HORSES
—— Rescue and Welfare ——

Registered Charity Number: 1075601
Bransby, Lincoln, LN1 2PH Telephone (01427) 788464
Website: www.bransbyhorses.co.uk Email: mail@bransbyhorses.co.uk

Bransby Horses is a registered charity, founded by Mr Peter Hunt in 1968 which has provided safe permanent refuge to over 1000 horses, ponies, donkeys and mules since it was established. Always concerned about the welfare of horses, Mr Hunt rescued his first horse in 1947, Sally a 4-year-old mare was being kept on a bombsite in South London. Broken in at 18 months and used to pull logs from a spinney, Sally was found tearing around a yard with a tyre round her neck after the furniture van she was kept in had overturned in a storm. Mr Hunt rescued her for £14 and rented a stable for her for 2/6 a week. When Mr Hunt moved to Bransby to start the charity Sally came with him.

Today the Home cares for over 500 rescued equines in our two centres, the main site being situated in the hamlet of Bransby, some eight miles from the historic city of Lincoln. Over 600 acres of land and four stable yards provide the best of specialised equine care for over 270 residents. Many come to us after being found abandoned, mistreated or neglected or because their owner can no longer care for them.

Our second centre, The Priory in Stoke Prior, Herefordshire was bequeathed to the charity in 2003. It had previously been run as a rescue centre for over 30 years by Arthur and Joyce Hall, friends of Mr Hunt, who established the centre having rescued 18 bakery horses that were being sold due to mechanisation. After extensive renovation the site now runs to over 80 acres and houses over 100 horses and is proudly able to continue the work started by the Halls. The centre is based in a prime location to help Welsh Mountain ponies; often ownerless and homeless these animals are left to fend for themselves under bleak conditions. Our staff provide a valuable service by monitoring the herds of ponies, supplying hay during the winter months and providing safe refuge to any animals that require specialist care.

We have a further 150 horses, ponies and donkeys that are placed in private homes under our re-homing scheme whereby they remain the property of the charity. The charity depends entirely upon donations and legacies for it to continue with its work.

Carrot and Spud's Story

Carrot and Spud arrived at the Home in September 2009, after a phone call from one of our supporters, who had asked for our help in providing a safe refuge for two thin elderly horses. Their rescue had been made possible due to members of public, who had become aware of their plight due to a photo of them being posted on the Horse and Hound forum. Both were desperately thin, with ribs and hip bones protruding from their weak bodies. Carrot was in such poor condition that we had huge reservations that he was going to make a full recovery. However, the way he came storming out of the lorry late that evening and objected to having his 'weigh in' gave us all hope that maybe he had the 'fighting spirit' to prove us wrong.

Months of specialised rehabilitation followed and the two boys made a complete recovery to health and in January 2010 we were overjoyed when we received the news that they had been signed over to Bransby for retirement. We were truly grateful and amazed for all the help that was offered both financially and in the messages of support that we received from their 'fan group'.

Carrot and Spud, both of whom are now in the early 30's, will be provided with the best of care and a secure home for the rest of their days, along with the other 500 residents at our two rescue centres.

Carrot and Spud are just two of many hundreds of equines that have come through our doors here at Bransby that have needed our help, which is only made possible by the kind generosity of those who donate to our work. People like Karen, who has kindly donated the proceeds of this book to Bransby to carry on rescuing horses in need.

From all the residents a huge thank you.

Prologue

My name is Hovis and I guess I'd better start at the beginning, because although this book has a beginning it's not THE beginning. The beginning was a year before this Diary starts, the day I met my Mum and Dad.

It's probably worth mentioning that a short time before I met Mum I'd been brought over from the Emerald Isle of my birth to a place in a hollow in Derbyshire. Here I was hanging out with a bunch of other dudes, generally chilling and waiting to be picked by our new Mums and Dads....

On the day in question I was down the field hanging out, admiring the mud pack I'd liberally applied and discussing the meaning of life with an older dude from Ireland who I think might have been a few sandwiches short of a picnic. Due to his randomness I was quite pleased to be dragged out of the field by the nice girl who looked after us and frog marched back to the yard. On route I was informed that a nice lady had come to see another horse and didn't like her so now she wanted to see me. Well I have to say that put my back up – I was only second choice to this woman huummm?

I got to the yard and was unceremoniously dumped into a room with a big window and was scrubbed down to within an inch of my life. It was the first time I had experienced this and it was to prove ironic as I have since spent most days avoiding Mum and a scrubbing brush....

Then soggy and dripping I was taken out to meet these people. The big strapping man with the big hands and the kind eye and the short, well conditioned, heavily boned, wild maned woman who wanted to look at me. The woman who was to become my Mum.

We went into the school and had a good hoon about which was fun as it was quite clear to me she had no control, no clue and didn't seem that bothered about flying around corners on two legs. She did however seem to have a problem with her breathing - although at the time I put this down to her having hay up her nose. I was later to discover when Mum is scared she sounds like Poof the magic dragon in need of an ambulance....

After a whizz round in the school we then went out for a hack and I obviously didn't scare her too much as when we got back she said she loved me and she wanted me.

So that was that. After enduring a "vetting" test (which the lads on the yard told me how to pass), having all my fur and feathers shaved off (I was NOT happy about that - I looked like I'd been scalped by a lawnmower) I was put on a really really big lorry and set off to my new home.

I came off the lorry, stood on my new Dads foot, slobbered all over my new Mum and realised there was a LOT of lovely ladies about. I was home.

In the year between this day and when my Diary starts, Mum, Dad and I got to know each other:

I realised that Mum standing tugging at my foot actually means she wants me to lift them up. She realised that when I don't want to pick my foot up she's not strong enough to make me.

I got the idea that sometimes I have to lift my feet up off the ground and jump over things. Mum did not get the idea whilst I'm quite good at it she still has to hang on tight.

Mum nicknamed me "The Destroyer" because I have "the turning circle of the Arc Royal". I adopted the name "The Destroyer" because it sounds manly and macho.

My Aunties named me "The Daffodil Destroyer" as I stomp on yellow things. This became shortened to "The Destroyer" for ease

It became clear to me that Dad is the brave one. Mum admitted Dad is the brave one although I think she prefers the term "fearless and brainless"?

And I realised how lucky I have been to get such a lovely home. Mum agreed.......

So this Diary picks up a year to the weekend that I arrived at my new home. Mum suggested I wrote it to keep a record of our time together so that's what I've done. Everything that happens in it has really happened to me, all the people I've met are really a part of my life and all the things Mum, Dad and I have done we've done together.

I hope you enjoy it...........

17.11.2008

Dear Diary
This last weekend I have been with my Mum for 1 year. She said it was our one year anniversary, I wasn't sure who Anni was but I liked the likit she bought me. Mum didn't seem to like it when I tried to share my likit and called me some rude names - some people are so ungrateful.

So I tried to think of something else to give her. I've had a week off as I have hurt my back and I need my saddle adjusting so yesterday I thought Mum might like to play tug of war. We were lunging and so I cantered off with her on the other end of the lunge line. The first time I think she liked it as she fell over with excitement but then when I did it again she had a funny expression on her face and really dug her feet in. I don't know why she did that as it ruined the whole point of the game and she called me even more rude names.

So what else to get her? When I get my saddle adjusted tomorrow I thought I could run really fast for her on a hack. When I've done that before she squeals with excitement and says fun things like "slow down you big fat bugger". My brother tells me that's not a term of endearment but I'm not so sure?

She's so hard to get presents for- she doesn't seem to appreciate hay down her back, or on her hair, she doesn't like me trying to carry her coat for her and when I tried to pour her tea out of her cup for her this morning she said I was going to be a pritt stick if I did that again (I take it that's a bad thing?) So any ideas of what to buy her to say thanks for our first year together?

05.12.2008

Dear Diary.
This week I have improved my vocabulary which I think is good. Mum says learning new things improves my pea like brain so I'm sure she's really pleased with me.

The new words include donkey, dipstick, pritt stick, yoohoo, dog food and chum. I also think you have to use a choice of symbols - ***, $$$, £££ and !!! - in front of all these words when you use them. It's all very exciting.

This week it's been very cold so Mum has put my thicker PJs on to sleep in. My brother has matching ones so I personally think we look gay. I have now decided that this may be the reason that the fit mare opposite doesn't return my come hither advances - she must think I'm making eyes at the gelding next to her. I was very hot the other morning so my brother was helping me take my PJs off when Mum walked in. Now I was very pleased to see her as it meant she could take them off for me instead as she's a bit more gentle but she seemed a little upset with us both. I'm not sure why - maybe she was in season?

That morning she was very slow getting us ready so Omar and I were trying to help her hurry up, I picked her gloves up for her and Omar drank that stuff she has to have each morning on her behalf. You'd think she'd be grateful but she used some of my new words of the week and took the gloves off me - I was only holding them!

I am SO misunderstood sometimes - the other day I was helping warm the stable cat up - how else am I supposed to blow on her without opening my mouth? Ok Omar told me that it DID look like I was trying to eat her but he is half TB so I'm not sure I trust his opinion.

Anyway as a special treat for Mum as she is always moaning about my feathers being dirty I have tried really hard to not walk in puddles. Is she grateful? Nope. She called me a fairy and smacked me with the lead rope. It was only because Omar copied me and she got squished. He's such a wuss and a teachers pet. To make up for squishing her I tried to help her hold Omar's head collar whilst she got it undone but apparently that was why we all got tangled up. It was great fun and afterwards when Omar and I went for our jog to suss out the laaddiiees we said what a fun morning we'd had. I love my Mum. I am however worried that she might not love me this week - I asked wise old Timmy tonight what "chum" meant as Omar told me it meant friend. Timmy asked if Mum said the word "pedigree" before she said chum. I think she did. Apparently that doesn't mean she's my friend it means dog food. I am a little confused.
Till next week Diary.......

12.12.2008

Dear Diary
This week Mum has hurt her knee. Apparently she slipped on the ice taking the short hairy thing that barks for a walk. This has meant she's not ridden me this week and has walked about with a thing that looks like one of my travel boots on her leg. I have tried to tell her she looks silly and have even tried to take it off for her a

few times but I don't think she was too amused. Nor did she laugh when I dropped hay down her and it got stuck to the Velcro bits. I bet she had hours of fun getting that off!

Whilst I didn't want Mum to hurt herself I was rather pleased as this meant I could have the week off chilling in the field and thinking what I'm going to buy the fit mare for secret Santa. Alas Mum had other ideas and other people have ridden me all week. OTHER people!

I have done my best to make sure they never want to ride me again though! I have bucked, napped, leaned on their hands and generally been rather naughty. This I figured would ensure that no one other than Mum rides me again. It seems though that this has angered Mum and so she's getting everyone to ride me to "get me used to it". I don't want to get used to it - that's the point. Wise Timmy told me last week (when Mum was mad with me) that to make sure she can never sell me I have to prove unrideable for anyone else. I am beginning to doubt the old mans wisdom as all it has achieved is me being worked to death every night. My life is SO pants.

So Diary to my biggest problem this week. What to get the fit mare for a pressie. I thought about giving her the shampoo my Mum bought for me that makes me smell like a fairy but will she think that I think she smells bad?

I thought about giving her some of my hay but she has that Fancy haleage stuff that Mum won't let me have so I think she's a bit high maintenance (I heard Dad say that about Mum once and I think it means they prefer posh hay). The only other option was the likit Mum got me the other day - only problem is I ate it. Do you think a salt lick says I care or that I'm a cheap skate?

22.12.2008

Dear Diary
I couldn't write to you on Friday as Mum was at some place called Olympia so I couldn't use the computer.

This week has been full of ups and downs.

I've not been feeling well as I've been having horrible vet people coming and putting stuff on my chest that really hurts. Mum says it's to get rid of a sarcoid on my chest but it really hurts and I don't like it. Mums being really kind to me but still I wish they'd stop doing it.

The upside is I've finally pulled fit mare!! Yeee haaa! Watch out boys there's a new player in town and he's called the Destroyer!

She's hurt her leg so has had to stay in which she doesn't like much. On Saturday after they'd come to put the horrible cream on me Mum left me in with fit mare as company for her. Just me, her and an empty barn…….. made for making a move and make one I did! I've leant her my treat ball and I soothed her nerves all day. Then on Saturday night on the way out of the barn she let me have a kiss. Hubba hubba that girl is HOT!

But now I have a problem. My new status as the yard Romeo (give them a treat ball and a neck nibble and they just roll over baby) is causing an issue. Next door to fit mare is another mare that lets just say isn't so fit. She's always scowling, showing off bad teeth and has breath that would knock you over at ten paces. Apparently in a few days time it's that thing called Kissmuss again and I have to give her a snog. Is this true? I really don't want to kiss her – she's well scary.

On a final note, women are complicated. That's my big lesson of 2008. The other week Mum shouted at me for getting my feathers dirty. This week when I went out for a hack with Aunty S (fit mares Mum) and came back filthy Mum said she was really proud of me. Go figure? Timmy says it's because I behaved myself brilliantly but I'm not sure he's to be trusted. He also says I have to snog the not-so-fit mare but how come he doesn't have to kiss her if it's Kissmuss? Are they taking the mick out of me?

28.12.2008

Dear Diary

'Twas the night before Christmas and all through the barn not a creature was stirring except for the not-so-fit mare. At first I thought she had something stuck in her teeth but then I realised she was blowing kisses at me. I was scared for my life……..

At midnight Mum said I had to bow down on one knee so like the good boy I am I did. When I glanced around though no one else was doing the same so I tried to cover it up by retrieving a bit of carrot I'd dropped earlier but somehow I think some of the others saw me as there was a fair bit of sniggering for the next hour or so. I think I looked silly in front of the fit mare so I was NOT happy.
On kissmuss morning Mum bought me a lovely lickit which I was to leave alone until kissmuss day night. Unfortunately the not-so-fit mare came past and caught me

unawares. Yuck yuck yuck!! She tasted HORRIBLE! Scary yuck yuck. Her breath was SO bad I forgot what Mum had said and stuck my nose in my lickit to get rid of the taste. Mum then didn't seem to appreciate my thank you kiss as much as she normally does. I have no idea why..... she looked good with war paint on and she smelt yummy.

On kissmuss day night my grandparents came to see me. I thought my Mum looked quite hassled and she muttered something to me about biting my grandma. She didn't come close enough though so I couldn't. Mum baffles me sometimes - normally I get a slapped nose for biting people.

I am confused - Omar says that it doesn't take much. He also says I am gullible. What does that mean? Mum calls me lots of things but never gullible. He's not trying to chat me up is he?

But my question this week dear Diary is what to wear for the new year party? Mum bought me a cool black rug which is nice but I think it shows off my belly too much. The other option is a blue rug but I think I look like a big Poof in it. Help what to do?

16.01.2009

Dear Diary

I'm sorry I haven't been a good boy and haven't been writing my Diary but will try harder from now on. Mum says we are now in a new year - what happened to the old one? Is it like my lickit i.e. it just disappears?

Mum hasn't be able to ride me as much recently as she has hurt her knee but other people have been teaching me new things for her. The evil woman who bosses Mum around made me go over trotting poles the other day that were OFF the ground! Wow! How do they do that? I wasn't too impressed though - does she not know how hard it is to lift legs my size up that far? Sheesh! I did it though so Mum gave me a polo not that that was a true indication of how hard I'd worked.

My brother continues to be annoying. A big Poof one minute then all brooding for the girls the next. Why can't I be 17.2HH and all handsome? Mum says that I've got a gorgeous face and a great personality but Timmy says that's what humans say about ugly people. Am I ugly then? Mind you at the minute I think I am ugly. Mum decided to give me a "tidy up" the other night. Does "tidy up" mean make you look like a schumck? She claims she got "distracted" and pulled too much of my fringe so I now look like a basin head. The fit mare told me I look like Friar tuck which since she was sniggering I don't think is a compliment. Is Mum trying to ruin my love life on purpose? First calling me silly names, then buying me poncey rugs and now making me look like a walking bog brush.

Mind you I may have a new development on the love life front. I think deep down the fit mare is a tart and is playing with me. Mind you I like being her toy - hubba hubba. But the foal I noticed the other day is starting to get all leggy and quite cute. Because she's younger than me she thinks I'm quite cool when I talk to her. So I'm thinking she might be worth investing some time in? Mum says I am a naughty cradle snatcher - is that wrong?

Oh PS I bit the farrier on the bum last night so Mum says I'm in the dog house. Does anyone know where the dog lives so I know where to sleep tonight?

22.01.2009

Dear Diary

I have to write to you today as Mum is going away this weekend and leaving me with Dad. Dad is not as much of a pushover as Mum so I don't think he'll let me borrow the computer.

This week has been fun - it's been really muddy and wet so me and my mate Bert have been doing mean slides from one side of the field to the other. Yeehaa! Mum however has been in a really bad mood with me. I don't know why. I thought if I tried to turn myself the same colour as big Poofball brother she'd be pleased. But NO! She shouted at me and called me a dosey pillock. What's a pillock?

This morning she let me into the field and said I had to behave. Well I tried. Really I did but the ponies were on the other side of the fence so Bert and I just HAD to have a race over to them. The last time I saw Mum this morning she seemed a little stressed - I don't know why? She was muttering about glue and pritt sticks so maybe she had to go home to mend something?

I am also in trouble because I broke that leg thing on one of my rugs - it wasn't my fault we were playing "I am the stallion" and it snapped. To make up for it I pulled my fleece off the hook last night and tried to dye it the same colour as my rug had been. Strangely Mum was mad about this too and mentioned the dog house again. I wish she'd just tell me where this dog lives then I could go and visit like she keeps suggesting.

Apparently next week some photographer is coming to take piccies of me so when she gets back Mum is going to make me look pretty. Please can one of you explain to her I am a MAN! I don't want to look pretty - I want to look manly and butch. If she makes me wear that gay rug I am going on strike.

Finally dear Diary as Mum is away this weekend I thought I could have a chilled out weekend doing nothing more than working on browning up my remaining white bits and chatting up the foal. But NO Mum has arranged for me to work!! How mean is that? Will someone adopt me please?

30.01.2009

Dear Diary

This week has been another funny one. Mum has been doing lots of work on me with no stirrups on I think because of her leg. Its nice to have Mum riding me again but its really BORING! Luckily she also let another aunt ride me and let me do some jumping - yeeehaaa! I love jumping although its much better if they just let me get on with it. I'm a big boy now and I know what I'm doing.

On Tuesday Mum said I had to have a bath as someone was coming to take my photo on Wednesday so I couldn't look like she'd found me tethered at the side of the road. I do sometimes wonder about my Mum - I know she bought me from a yard so why would anyone think she'd bought me off the side of the road? Timmy says you buy flowers off the side of the road so I think Mum is getting confused.

On Wednesday morning Mum seemed a touch upset that one of my knees wasn't the lovely white it had been the night before. What did she expect me to do - levitate all night? She sprayed some stuff on to get me white again but it turned my knee purple just as the man came to take my piccie. She then told me that I was going to be FAMOUS!! Wow! Ha the fit mares ears lifted at that I can tell you.

So did my brothers though which was not so good. So Mum and I had to have a cuddle and then do some riding whilst this man took photos then my brother came in and he took some pictures of us together. Its so UNFAIR!! My moment of fame and he's muscled in. Anyway ALL the girls have chatted me up ever since so I think this fame thing could be good for the love life.

Mum has said how proud she was of me and we've been really cuddly all week. Until this morning..........

My brother wears this really stupid neck warmer thing and for the last few days I've been taking it off for him. We've usually waited till Mum leaves then we've taken it off and hid it. But this morning he wanted it off straight away and as I took the Velcro straps off Mum turned around. She was REALLY mad! Then she smacked ME on the bum - how come its my fault?!! He ASKED me to take it off. He let her put it back on again but then came over to me to take it off again before Mum had completely gone - I TOLD him she's got eyes in the back of her head. Now we're BOTH in trouble and Omar's neck is going to get cold as Mum took it off him. HA!

So does anyone know if they do double rooms in the dog house? And what does "selling the bl**dy both of you as a job lot" mean?.....

06.02.2009

Dear Diary
This week has been SO boring. On Sunday night all this white stuff fell out of the sky and covered everything so we're not allowed to go out. I guess this white stuff kills horses?

It was Mums birthday on Monday so Dad and the girls decorated my stable for her. I don't see why they had to decorate my stable - why couldn't they decorate her bed? So when they had gone I took all the streamers down - Mum seemed to find this funny though so that was fine.

They did leave this strange thing behind that floated in the air. It was a very clever thing because when I tried to get hold of it, it floated out of the way. Poofy brother Omar was scared of it at first but when it didn't eat me he tried to help me catch it. It was really hard and we tried for HOURS but the little thing was too clever for us. Mum took it away with her when she came down that night so maybe its in the dog house now for not playing with us?

The rest of the week we've all been stuck inside although Mum did sneak us out for a couple of hours the other day. It has been really boring but has given me a chance to chat up the fit mare. She is seriously high maintenance but I can forgive her when she has such gorgeous legs.

Mum has filled my treat ball up every day for me to play with but I keep getting in trouble for being so loud with it. Look people I am a very very big boy, I have big legs and HUGE feet (you know what I'm saying ladies?!) so like DUH of course when I kick it about I'm going to make a noise! How else do I get the treats out of the thing?

Mum said yesterday she's seen the proof from our photo shoot and I look yummy. I wish she wouldn't say things like that in front of the fit mare. She spent all night sniggering and singing "your Mummy thinks you're yummy, you're going to end up in her tummy". So not funny. Mums not going to eat me is she?

Anyway she says she looks like a total twerp but I look handsome so I'm cool with that. When its out ladies you know where to come - its Destroyer time! Anyway I've now had enough of this white stuff so today I have organised for all of us to lean over our doors and breathe really hard to defrost the ice. Do you think it will work?

20.02.2009

Dear Diary

I am so very sorry for not writing to you last week. There was no computer in the dog house and that's where I was.

I was allowed out on Saturday to let young Amy ride me but nearly ended up straight back in the dog house again. Ok so I made a big deal about the banging noise and after I realised I wasn't about to be killed I could have stopped tanking around the ménage like a loon but Amy was laughing so I carried on. Mum however was not laughing and yelled at me - now when she uses THAT tone I stop. Very suddenly. Its what she wanted me to do so why it was my fault Amy ended up round my ears I have NO idea.

Anyway then we did some poles and things and I was having a ball.... until they turned the last pole into a jump without telling me. There I was looking down admiring the way my feathers were wafting in the breeze when WHOA JUMP!! I did take it a bit high I must admit but heh I cleared it.

Next time round I was ready for it and jumped as soon as I got over the pole on the ground. Now it did seem a bit of a long way away but heh if that's what I am to do then fine. Mum by this time was crying with laughter so I'm not sure what I'd done. Apparently the pole was 11 human strides away from the jump but that doesn't mean a lot to me - Mum has short legs.

I went out for a hack with one of my Aunties this week too. That was fab fun. I went out in front because Poof bags was scared and my auntie said she was surprised how brave and fast I am. Heh lady I AM the Destroyer - you know what I'm saying?!!

But the biggest problem of the week dearest Diary is once again women. Since we've moved fields I get to hang out over the fence talking to the ponies and the yard managers school mare. Now she's a sweet very solid, normal type. She's rather keen on me I think so I think its a sure thing. Mum likes her and says she's a much better match than fit mare. But fit mare is FIT. All legs and attitude. Mum says she's a tart and I have to agree but heh I don't want to take her home to my parents you know? So what do I do? Go with the solid dependable girl who my Mum likes or keep chasing the fittest thing on 4 legs I've ever seen? PS Can someone have a word with the owner of the dog house and ask why they don't serve carrots there?

PPS Can someone also tell Mum to let me grow my fringe out rather than retrimming it to the bowl shape she's already given me. I can't even pull a toilet chain let alone a mare if I look like friar tuck.

27.02.2009

Dear Diary
Where do I get a passport? I've decided I wish to move to France, get bought by a nice British person then be allowed to never work again in a field in Norfolk. Anything has got to be better than the amount of work Mum has made me do this week.

I honestly think I am a good candidate for an exciting RSPCA rescue from this evil woman. Twice this week she has made me go out to work BEFORE she has filled my haynet!!! How am I supposed to wedge hay behind my bit if there's none there when she tacks me up? HONESTLY!

Anyway despite mother working me into the ground this week has been good. My best mate Bert has come back from the vets so I've got a field buddy again.

Poof bags Omar and his little creep friend don't play with me as much as Bert so I've missed him. Mum however hasn't missed us boys play fighting as I keep coming in with various bite marks and scratches and she goes MAD! Apparently if I scar myself up much more she can't even tie me to the roadside to get rid of me. Personally I think it makes me look much more manly.
This week Poof bags and I have had to have words. Its bad enough that fit mare drools over him like he's a mint lickit but now he's chatting up nice solid mare. Now the boy needs to decide which girl he wants - I don't mind having his cast offs but he's not having both of them. At this rate I'm going to have to start chatting up the foal again.

Mum has told me this week that in June we're all going away to the sea side for the weekend. I'm not sure what the sea side is? Wise Timmy says it is this thing you sit on and it goes up and down which doesn't sound much fun? BUT fit mare is coming with us. The bad news is so is Poof bags but heh I can dream. She says we have to take our swim suits so not sure if this thing that goes up and down dunks you under water? It sounds like a sheep dip to me? So I'm thinking do I pack the speedos or the big baggy shorts? Timmy says I should ask Mum for a mankini but he sniggered when he said it so not sure if he's trying to make me look silly?

Anyway I've got a while to plot my moves so I will sleep on it.

In the meantime if anyone whose Mum doesn't work them really hard fancies swapping places for a few weeks that would be cool. Man I need a holiday!

06.03.2009

Dear Diary

I am FAMOUS. Or so Mum tells me. I'm not sure what it means as she seems happy that I am famous but Timmy says it means I fart too much? How is this a good thing?

I'm not sure if the two things are related but man has my pulling power suddenly increased! Yesterday I got pounced on by the fairly fit ginger mare and snogged! Tongues and EVERYTHING! Woowee!! Then she and very fit mare fought over me! Wow! How cool is that! I can tell you I strutted down to my field like a prince. I AM the man!

Mum however did not think I was the man at the weekend. I'd gone out with my Aunty and Poof bags when we came across these terrifying little yellow things. I vaguely remember they tried to invade last year and they're back! Yikes they are SO scary. They lie in the grass waiting to pounce on you and EAT you. I tried to save my Aunty by rushing through them and trying to get as far away as possible. Poof bags obviously knows about them eating us too as he did the same thing. For some reason my Aunty and Dad didn't seem thankful that we had saved them and told us both off. How ungrateful. Mum is muttering something about buying plastic flowers but I'm not sure why. If this is another harebrained scheme she has picked up off these internet forums there will be trouble.

Anyway I must go and pose some more by the fence. Children came this morning and took photos of me so this fame thing is cool. They gave me polos and didn't give Poof bags any so his very handsome nose is rather out of joint. Ha!

Does this fame thing mean I don't have to do any work though?

13.03.2009

Dear Diary

This week has been another fun one. I went out at the weekend with Aunty Sarah and Poof bags again and she was most impressed with me. After last weeks issues with the yellow invading things I did try to save her again but gave up when she told me off. If she wants to get us killed then that's fine I can't seem to get her to understand.

Mum brought the bodies of the yellow invading things and showed them to me the other day. I wasn't bothered by them because they were DEAD. Its when they're creeping through the grass towards you that they're dangerous. Honestly Mum is SO dense sometimes. Mind you I obviously did something right as there was much patting and treats when she put them near me. Why I should be bothered by dead yellow things I have NO idea.

This fame thing carries on reaping rewards. I got extra carrots and an apple on Tuesday when one of my other Aunties came over. Plus ginger mare is still flirting like mad!Ha! Poof bags is SO put out. Mind you he got a big fuss made of him the other day because he jumped a jump without freaking out! What's that all about? I could jump that with my eyes closed - although probably not a good idea because one of us out of Mum and I ought to look where we're going.............

Mum and I made a break through the other night. since she hurt her knee and has to wear a funny travel boot on her leg I have problems knowing sometimes if she's still on board. When I can't feel her leg on me I slow down to go back and check if she's fallen off then she gets all upset. However the other night evil woman gave her a little silver thing for her foot and I could feel that so all was cool. We had the best hoon round the ménage we've had in ages!
I was in trouble though yesterday - me and the boys had been playing pretty hard and I'd cut all my mouth. It didn't hurt much and made me look very manly but Mum was FUMING!! She called me all sorts of rude names as apparently the cut was where my flash goes. I didn't see what the problem was personally but I have a feeling if I do I again I'll be back to the casa del pero (d'ya like that - I've been told an accent works wonders with the ladies?!!!)

20.03.2009

Dear Diary
Do you think I will get frequent visitor points for the amount of time I spend in the dog house?

I seem to have been in trouble a lot this week.

First off when Auntie Sam and I went out with Poof bags and fit mare at the weekend. We did a lot of cantering which I love and I was impressing fit mare with my speed. Now I admit I was getting a bit excited (I love going fast) but at no point was I running away with her. How was I supposed to know what "slow down you big hairy person-of-unknown-parentage" means? She could have tried a simple "whoa!" AND it was her idea to jump the cross country jump with me - I just like to go at it a bit faster than she obviously liked. She was laughing by the time we got back but Mum says if I keep acting like a tank no one will want to ride me.

I think fit mare was impressed though! Talking of mares what's with the ladies at the moment. Geez! I am in 7th heaven. They are THROWING themselves at me. Admittedly they seem to be throwing themselves at everyone but I'm not complaining. Mum is though as I do need to stop in a morning and talk to the laadies. Apparently I am pulling her arms out. Well let go then DUH! The final issue was with the head collar box. Mum has bought a big yellow box to keep our head collars dry at the gate. Now she seems to think I am scared of anything yellow (which I am not!). So the other morning I put my head under the fence, dragged the box into the field, tipped it over and threw all the head collars out. Now I thought she'd be pleased with my bravery but she called me a rude name. Honestly there is NO pleasing the woman.

So all in all whilst I have been an angel with Mum in the school all week I still think I'm in the dog house. Anyone want to join me?

26.03.2009

Dear Diary
Yesterday I lost my best friend. Lost is a silly word because I know where he is, Mum has told me, and I know he's not coming back.

So I raise a hoof and a glass to you Bertie, I'll miss you.
I'll miss you;
Because you were always grumpy in the morning and made me laugh biting people when they weren't looking
Because you had the biggest yawn in the world.
Because you helped me pull our rugs down to make our Mums mad.
Because you shared your hay and stole mine.
Because you always wanted to beat me to the field but called to me as I walked down the lane.
Because no matter how long after you I got there, you always waited for me by the gate.
Because we'd stand together at the drinking trough, shoulder to shoulder and dribble water down our chins.
Because you'd run with me to the gate when my Mum came to fetch me.

Because if she wasn't bringing you in as well, you'd hang on to my tail and not let go.
Because even when you were in pain you'd play with me for hours.
Because you were calmer if I stood with you when you were down in the field and couldn't get up.

But most of all I'll miss you because you were my best friend and the field is empty without you.

RIP big grey man.
When my time one day comes, wait for me at the gate.

03.04.2009

Dear Diary

Firstly I must start with an apology. It appears that my father and Poofbags have discovered my guilty pleasure and have been posting on the Horse and Hound online forum insulting fellow "generously built" types. I am SO sorry. He is an ignorant pig.

Mind you he's not had a good week *snigger*. Firstly he has a pathetic cough and seems to think he is dying. Honestly he is SUCH a drama queen. Then Dad has been trying to get him to load on the lorry.

Well honestly I've never seen anything like it. Shaking and running away from a LORRY! Its hardly going to eat him is it? So one night Dad decided to ask if I would stand on the lorry to convince Poof bags that it wasn't THAT bad. So like a good little boy I did. But he took so long to summon up the courage I got bored so I waited till he was nearly on, standing nice and quietly then just as he got on I kicked the wall! Hee Hee! He nearly wet himself, jumped up, banged his head on the roof and ran away! Dad was furious with me but Mum was laughing. I think she thinks Poof bags is a wuss too.

This week I've got a new posh saddle too! Mum says that the last one was too small for her so she couldn't pull back enough to stop me. Why she would want to stop me I have no idea but heh if it makes her happy! Its dark brown and very trendy - I'm getting a new bridle and things as well so I guess I'd better stop rubbing my head on things whilst wearing it.

I had a night jumping with aunt L again this week which was great fun and an opportunity to spend time with fit mare. Her and Poof bags had a "moment" last weekend which I think has convinced her finally he doesn't like girls. She'd been giving him the come on all the way around a hack but when they got back he bit her lip and called her a tart! She turned round and gave him both back legs and he did the same to her! How RUDE! So I might be back in there. Nice normal mare is kind of put out with me but how can I resist legs that long and eyelashes to die for?!!

Life is so hard sometimes!!

13.04.2009

Dear Diary
Sorry for the delay to my weekly entry but Mum has been making me do stupid things all weekend so I couldn't get near the computer.

Apparently its a thing called Easter this weekend - what the heck its for I have NO idea but it has made all the humans behave most oddly.

But first to the last week. Diary I think I have to finally admit defeat with fit mare. I think its my brother she lusts after and she uses me to make him jealous. I am so upset that she prefers that prancing Poof of a brother of mine to me - I know he's taller than me, darker and all brooding but seriously he'd be no good in the woods defending her from the green and red dive bombers (Mum says they're called peasants but I think she's just being rude).

So I have to say I've been mostly depressed this week. Nice and "normal" mare hasn't forgiven me for chasing the long legged tart in preference to her more curveous charms so I am worried that I'm going to be left on the shelf.

Anyway I must pull myself together or wise Timmy will bite my bum again. Talking of biting I am in trouble AGAIN!! Mum was grooming me the other day so I thought she'd like it if I groomed her at the same time. The problem was she smelt all nice and lemony and for a split second I forgot it was Mum and took a bite. She squarked like a startled mare in season and called me all sorts of rude names. I admit the black and blue mark on her arm is rather large but I'm not sure she needed to make THAT much fuss.

So I think this EASTER thing has been her revenge. We've all been dragged out by our humans to go EGG hunting?!!! Do I look like a chicken? Why would I want an egg? And more importantly why would I want to find it? I didn't lose it so why is it my job to find it? So yesterday we all trooped out whilst our humans faffed about reading something called a "glue" which apparently told them where the egg was. If they're being told why did we have to go? Mind you I was worried for my Mum when we found ours as a big white plastic monster had eaten the egg and Mum tried to rescue it. I wasn't so sure this was a good idea so in the end Mum got off the safety of my back and braved the creature alone. She then called me a Poof. EXCUSE me - Poofbags didn't even get to come out of his stable as Dad knew he'd be no use at all. Anyway most other humans came back on foot so I obviously wasn't the only one worried about the white creatures. They all seemed to have had fun so that's ok.

Anyway that's enough from me - I'm off to sob broken heartedly into my hay net whilst pretending to have a cold. I HATE girls.

17.04.2009

Dear Diary
This week has been most confusing.

First of all Mum has announced I have to stop growing or she'll stop feeding me. How on earth do I STOP growing? I'm not TRYING to grow it just seems to be happening? Someone please help me with some suggestions as I like my brekkie and tea - especially tea as Mum puts stinky garlic in it - yum! Life will be so boring if I can't eat anymore - Mum said she'd sew my mouth up but wise Timmy says someone would report her to horseline if she did that. PHEW!

But the most confusing thing has been fit mare. This week I have been on two romantic walks in the woods with her! Just her and me walking side by side in the sunshine. I am in 7th heaven! But I have no idea if she's playing with me. On Weds she looked at me all longingly - or so I thought - Poof bags said she had something in her eye. So what do I do? If I carry on chasing the fit long legged one nice normal mare will never forgive me and then if fit mare goes back to Poof bags I am alone again. What to do?

Poof bags meanwhile has been behaving like an embarrassing tart. He and fit mare keep standing in the field staring at each other over the fence. THEN the other day he laid on his back with his bum towards her, legs in the air, DISPLAYING himself!!!! I was SO embarrassed!

To my young mind it was SO inappropriate to show yourself to a girl like that but ladies is that what you like? Is that what I'm going to have to do to win fit mare? Show her my Hovis sausage?

I can't ask Mum - can you IMAGINE how embarrassing that conversation would be? So please ladies - HELP me!

24.04.2009

Dear Diary
What a lovely week this week has been. Its been all nice and warm and sunny so we've all been out naked. Even Poof bags. That was the good bit. The bad bit was that Mum decided it was time for the first bath of the year. Yuck! Why does she think its funny to make me smell like a lemon sherbet? She uses one of those poof type

18

things and lathers me up till I look like I've been in a washing machine. So there am I - hair plastered to my head, bubbles everywhere - when fit mare walks past. How can I look cool and sexy if I look like a poodle? So I shook myself to try to shake off the bubbles and seemed to manage to soak fit mare, her Mum and my Mum all at the same time. Oooops! That did NOT go down too well.

But my new lemony smell has had other benefits. There is a very expensive show jumping (SJ) mare on the yard that normally we never get to see as she lives in another field. BUT she's moved fields at the moment and I have to walk past her. Normally she doesn't even look at me but after my bath she cantered over and licked my neck. This was great until I remembered what I do when something smells all nice (i.e. bite it) she is rather yummy but even I know she's out of my league.

This week Mum has been doing loads of BORING schooling with me. Walk, sitting trot, rising trot, sitting trot, halt. Etc etc. YAWN! What happened to tanking along like a loon? BUT we're going cross country schooling tonight and Dad isn't taking Poof bags. I think that means he will ride me as well as Mum so I might get some tanking in tonight! It does mean I have to go on the lorry with ginger two-timing-wench mare but I might get to bite her as we drive along.

I'll let you know how I get on next week!!

01.05.2009

Dear Diary

This week has been a bit weird. Mum has been away for three days so Dad has been looking after me. I can't get away with things the way I can with Mum. BORING!!

But the highlight of the week was going cross country jumping last Friday night. I had to travel with ginger two-timing-wench mare but I tried my best to be nice to the slut. She is still playing hard to get after I caught her cheating on me with Poof bags so I ignored her most of the way there.

We got to the place and it was all very exciting! I was SO wanting to go and get on with it that Dad and I fell out about me standing still to be tacked up. If he'd hurried up a bit then we'd have been fine!

Question though why do Mum and Dad have to wear a suit of armour when we go to these places? They do look silly!

Anyway Dad rode me first - that's always fun as he likes to go REALLY fast! Apparently I was pulling like a steam train whatever that means but it was only because I wanted to get out there and play! It is SO much fun. Dad and I jumped logs, climbed up banks, jumped tyres and then ... well then came the problem. Dad wanted me to jump this thing called a coffin. I thought coffins are what they bury people in? I wasn't keen on this idea so as Dad and I trotted towards it I slammed the anchors on. Dad sailed up round my ears which was a little concerning but he stayed on. This coffin thing looked like the grand canyon!! No WAY was I risking my life and Dads trying to jump this thing. Anyway my desire to save Dads life didn't seem to go down well with him and he kept INSISTING we had to jump over this thing. So in the end (against my better judgement) we did. I did ensure our safety by jumping 6 ft in the air and 7ft wide. This tactic worked and we lived! Bugger me though not satisfied with this Dad made me do it again - several times. This is when I do think Mum has more brains.

Anyway after this terrifying experience we rode down to the water jump which I LOVE!! Its all smelly and wet! YUM! Then Mum got on me. We went paddling again and stood with ginger two timer as she was all scared and Poofy. Maybe that's why her and Poof bags like each other - they're both wimps. Note he wasn't there as he'd be too scared. I, however am a big brave tank. Mum and I played about for a while then Dad said we had to have a race through the woods with ginger wench. Well at least I think it was supposed to be a race - I ensured we won anyway just in case that was the desired outcome. I'm not being beaten by a spindly legged ginger thing. I was SO tired though by the end. Mum gave me extra tea and cuddles though so that was fab!

We might be going again next week but Dad says I have to stop pulling his arms out because he's starting to look like a gorilla. Mum says him looking like a monkey has nothing to do with me. I suggest next time he just lets go - I am a big boy and I know what I'm doing. Duh!

So I think this XC thing might be my forte (d'ya like that? "forte" - I am turning into a right walking dictionary). Basically you tank about a big field at top speed jumping over things. None of this poncing about with your nose on your chest which Poof bags does so well - oh no this is a sport where men are men and Poofy people stay in the stables. Yeeeh haa!

So until next week Diary, I wonder if someone can just explain why Mum says that she's going to have to rob the bank to pay for my shoes and things. I jumped OFF the bank on Friday and I saw no money anywhere? Eh?

08.05.2009

Dear Diary
This week Mum has been away again. I don't like her going away, Dad rides me and whilst he likes going really really fast (which is fun) he also shouts at me for pulling. I'm NOT pulling. I'm getting from a to b as fast as possible and his arms are slowing me down. It's not difficult.

He and Mum have started talking about putting me in a different bit to stop me so thought I'd throw them a curve ball. I let Dad ride me and pulled really hard, then the next day Mum was back and I was really soft and gentle with her THEN Mum let Aunty Sarah ride me and I rode all the way around the hack with my reins so loose I could have skipped with them. Ha! THAT confused Dad! Mum has told him it's him!! Hee Hee

When Aunt Sarah rode me weird things were happening in the field near the drive. These odd tent things appeared and they sacrificed a pig. The poor thing! They speared it with a big stick and then cooked it! I am SO worried about upsetting Mum now in case she does the same to me. I heard Uncle D say they'd have got more meat off me so yikes!

Apparently it was Uncle D's birthday and he was older than even wise old Timmy. Wow! That's OLD! I thought the only things that lived longer than Timmy were trees. Anyway that night all the humans stayed really late and kept us awake with embarrassing Mum and Dad type music. What's with listening to George Michael? I know Uncle D is old but is he deaf too? What's wrong with a bit of hard core drum and base? I was well annoyed with Mum as we all wanted to party and she and all the others kept popping in to make sure we were alright. Of course we're alright – we'd be even better if they had left.

The funniest sight though was the next day. It was really windy and these tent things started blowing about. I was in the stables waiting for the evil one to give Mum a lesson when WHOOSH! The tent thing took off! Next thing Mum and Aunty T jumped on it – it was so heroic! They saved the tent thing from being blown away. They did appear to want to cuddle the tent thing for a while as they held on to it for ages whilst shouting encouraging things like "bl**dy wind" "oh balls" and "who's stupid idea was this" – erm dumb question – theirs! I wanted to go and help as it looked like fun but Mum wasn't keen. Oh and for reference banging on the stable door to signal your Mum when she's cuddling a flying tent isn't the done thing apparently.

So this week Diary I am keeping my eyes peeled for anyone approaching me with a stick or any fires. Hovis burgers will NOT be on the menu - I don't care whose birthday it is!

15.05.2009

Dear Diary

Mum has been away again this week - boo hiss. I hate her being away. At the weekend Mum rode me on the Saturday which was really nice but I was so tired! We went for a walk afterwards with fit mare in the woods and I could hardly lift my feet up. This did mean that Mum seemed to keep ending up around my ears quite a lot. She might have been doing an ear inspection but judging by her language it might have had something to do with me falling over my own feet. Ooops.

So on Sunday I think she was getting her revenge. She made me have a bath in the middle of the yard with everyone watching. With COLD water. Horrible woman. She said it was because I was a itchy mitey mess but personally I think she just enjoys ruining any chance I have of pulling. How can I pull fit mare when I'm shivering and covered in smelly soap suds? Admittedly the shivering bit was me trying to garner some attention because it was quite warm. I also figured how to stop the water which did not go down well with Mum. Every time she turned round I stood on the snake which was spitting the water on me. That seemed to stop the thing spitting (which is SO rude) but Mum didn't seem amused. Well I find me funny.

I had a ride with Aunty S while Mum was away and then Mum came back and I dropped a boob. A BIG one. I dragged her all over the place the first night she was back trying to get some grass and she was REALLY mad at me. So she took me in that cage thing and made me run round and round. What she doesn't know is I've already figured if I drop my head, chew my mouth and stick my tongue out she lets me stop. But dammit I forgot the bit that after that I'm supposed to follow her around looking all sorry. Bugger! So she made me run round again. I'm such a duh! I was pooped by the time she'd finished! I love my Mum lots but sometimes she's plain odd.

Oh I forgot to add Poof bags and I had a tiff this week. I suggested his Mum might not have been a pure TB and he got VERY upset. Fortunately for me as he started to beat me up Mum and Dad came and he got told off! hee Hee! He is bigger than me though so I figure next time I'm going to tell him his Dad was a mongrel and then RUN really fast before he can bite me. Because when his perfectly Poofy teeth land on my bum it doesn't half hurt. Ouch!

22.05.2009

Dear Diary
Mum has been away AGAIN this week - boo. But this has meant Dad and I have been out hacking - yeeaaah!

The other day we went down to the river bank with fit mare. I love the river bank - we get to go really really fast flat out for a mile and a half. Cool! I was so excited but Dad was saying I couldn't go yet so I was dancing. Dad told Mum that I was piffying on the spot. I'm not sure what piffying is but Mum seemed to want to know why I can't do that in the school. Mainly because we can't get up to warp speed in the school so why would I have to dance? Anyway I was thrilled when fit mare turned round and said "eat my bum Hovis"! Finally! I'd done it! Pulled the long legged hot mama. But no! What she meant was she was going to shoot off at top speed and have me chase her. Well this was fine until she somehow had a turbo boost and I couldn't keep up! The thing that barks says there is a film where people have a turbo boost on their car and blue lights underneath it. I want one fitted. I'd look cool flying along with blue neon lights on my feathers. Timmy say that putting up coloured lights says I want people to pay me for sex. Which is SO not true.

I don't want them to pay me .... I'd do it for free if I could find anyone willing

Talking of which I am concerned I'm being eyed up to be the next meal ticket for a one parent mother. Timmys field mate is quite cute but then Timmy told me she's nearly 18 and has 5 children by 5 DIFFERENT men! What a slut! Even I daren't go there - I don't get enough pocket money to support that kind of family even if she might be able to teach me a thing or two.

So it looks like I continue with nice normal mare who kissed me yesterday. Mum was not amused as I stood with my bird at the opposite side of the field last night and wouldn't come in. Hey I was with my girl y'know. I still lust after fit mare though so I feel a bit naughty.

In other developments Poof bags has hurt himself. He fell over his own feet when hacking the other day and has cut his knees open. Poor diddums. Honestly the fuss that's being made. When I fall over my own feet Mum shouts at me. He's getting loads of attention and is lapping it up. Ha! He didn't think it was so funny to make a fuss when Mum and Dad called the vet and he had to have an injection in his bum. That'll teach him. He has got the weekend off work though so he'd better not make a move on my girl.

Oh and just one thing Diary. How do you hide singed feathers? I had back shoes put on for the first time this week and the farrier wasn't paying attention (too busy gossiping with Dad) and burnt a bit of my feather. They both thought this was funny and promised each other not to tell Mum. I showed her this morning though by picking my back leg up really high when she was picking my feet up. She was really mad. Never mind being mad! Does anyone know how to stop me looking like a part baked hedgehog?

28.05.2009

Dear Diary
I am exhausted. I'm over worked, under paid and under appreciated. I want a new Mum and Dad. I want a massage. I want a fit mare to lick me all over. I want to stay in bed today! Phew I feel better for that!

This week has been like boot camp. I have been worked into the ground – I feel so feeble I can barely type these words.

On Saturday Dad and I went on a hack with posh SJ mare, loony SJ boy and a couple of others. It was great fun but I wanted to be at the front. So I pulled Dads arms …..Quite a lot. Oooops. Big mistake. HUGE. I'll come back to why in a moment.

On Sunday Mum and I had a nice little ride and as usual I was as good as gold for her. I love my Mum even if she did then give me another bath. In the middle of the yard. With cold water. Apparently she had to (yeah right) because the stuff she put on me last week had to be put on again. Yeah right do I look like I was born in a bog in Ireland? Huum? Do people think I'm stupid?

On Monday the trouble started. Dad took me into the jumping paddock. Oh WOW!! I love jumping SO much. So ok I was a little strong but if he had just let me get on with it I'd got everything under control – all he had to do was sit there. In the end I'd had enough of him insisting he knew better than me so I started running away from the jumps. Ouch – note to self don't do that again. I was in BIG trouble. SO on Tuesday Dad and I went in there again. Fabby I thought! Alas no. These evil evil parents of mine have put something new in my mouth and boy I don't like it! I can't run away in it at all. How pants is that? Aunty Sarah jumped me too because Mum is away again and I've started to think she's a bossy mare as well. I like to go into a jump MY way not her way. Alas with this new horrible thing in my mouth she seemed to be stronger than me so I lost. Dad was really smug. I don't think it's funny. So last night we went to a COMPETITION!! I had to go with two-timing-ginger-wench mare again but I am started to think I might have judged her too harshly. From hereon in she is not-too-bad-even-if-she-is-ginger-wench mare. Anyway we got there and Dad tacked me up and took me into the warm up thingy. I don't like it in there so tried to take Dad out of there at top speed. But drat it! That damned metal thing stopped me again. So I figured if Dad wanted to die we might as well stay in there and work. So we jumped a few jumps and then we went into the big place.

I liked it in there and was quite happy until we went near this wall and people were in it! And a horse!! Who looked like me! How freaky! I didn't like that bit so when we came to jump the fence near there I ran away. Dad made me come back and jump it so I did and dashed to the next fence. After that all was fine and so we jumped everything else clear. I am such a clever boy!

Then Aunty Sarah jumped me and I just didn't pick my feet up over the fence near the scary horse that looked like me. I was too busy checking he wasn't behind the wall anywhere. But I decided this was all quite fun so I jumped all the others.

Aunty Sarah and Dad made a big fuss and gave me treats. Fab! Dad says Mum will be really proud of me. Which I love. Do you think she might take this thing out of my mouth so I can go fast again?

05.06.2009

Dear Diary

I am SO sorry I am late tonight Diary - Mum and Dad have been out for the day so I couldn't use the computer.

Well this week has been fun. After my exploits last week Mum gave me a few days off to recover and then she and Dad were away for the weekend so it gave me some bonding time with my new field mate. He's called Felix and is a lot bigger than me but seems ok. He's not Bert, no one will ever replace him, but he seems quite cool. Mum wasn't too keen when she saw what he's done to my face but I like playing "we're stallions" with him.

Mum was away again this week but Dad took me out on Tuesday for a hack. I was in 7th HEAVEN! I went with fit mare, expensive SJ mare and nice normal mare. Oh my lord. What was a boy to do?! The only one missing from my bevy of beauties was ginger-two-timing-wench mare but more on that later.
We went out for a nice trot and I tried to show off but dammit that stupid bit they've put me in has ruined my speedy capabilities! PANTS! At one point I had to take charge and be the MAN leading the way through the overgrown woodland. Omar said it was because they figured if I could fit through the gap then so could they but I think it was because the laaadies felt safe with me!

Mum came home on Thursday and we had a really lovely ride together. She was so gentle with me and I tried really hard. she was very proud of me. But the best of all was this morning.

After my girls and I had been out in the week news of my manliness has obviously spread! As Mum turned me round to shut my stable door this morning ginger-not-so-much-of-a-wench mare SNOGGED me!! Full on tongues! What do I do? Go for ginge who is a bit spindly but seems keen (but then 2 timed me with my brother), fit mare (who fancies my brother), expensive SJ mare (who is way way way out of my league) or nice normal mare?

26

Dad has told me today that we're going jumping again on Sunday so I might win a rosette? Ginger-maybe-I-quite-like-the-little wench will be coming too so maybe I can make a move in the lorry? So I'll keep you posted on both the jumping and the love life! Man it could be a good day!

PS Omar is all jealous so on Wednesday he tried to jump some jumps with Dad! He might be all tall, handsome and brooding but the Destroyer he isn't!!

12.06.2009

Dear Diary
I am in trouble. Again. I know this appears to be a regular thing but I don't mean to get in trouble it just happens. I'll explain in a bit.

Anyway the week started with Mum and Dad taking me back to that horrible place where the evil small ponies screamed at me so much I ran away (they were yelling that I didn't have my balls anymore and they did - it was HORRIBLE!) and Mum fell off.

It was raining, blowing a gale and I wasn't keen at all. Whilst the little screaming things could not be seen I wasn't too sure they weren't hiding somewhere. But Dad and I stayed in the little arena thing and eventually I decided they might have gone on holiday. Once I realised they weren't there I quite enjoyed myself and Dad and I jumped the jumps in the big arena twice. I did knock a couple down but Mum and Dad seemed very happy with me.

Then on Monday I got a real shock. I came in from the field with Dad and realised Timmy had shrunk! Big time! I know it had been raining but I didn't realise we could shrink in the wash? I was quite panic stricken until I realised it wasn't Timmy. My new next door neighbour is called Buttons, is very small, very fat and apparently itchy. I hope its not catching as every time I itch Mum makes me have a cold bath. He's very annoying, talks constantly and has pulled my rug off and wee'd on it. I was not amused. Dad wouldn't let me go round and sort him out but I'll get the little bugger. I'm not too sure I'm not allergic to him too. I've got quite a cough at the minute which is most annoying but fit mare and ginger-I-think-I-might-quite-like-gingers-wench mare seem to be keen to sooth my fevered brow. Not so Mum who has called the vet so no doubt they'll do something horrible to me later.

This week Omar has been giving me words of wisdom. He told me the grass is always greener on the other side. So never being one to disagree with my elders Felix and I leant over the fence to eat the grass from the other side. Do you see where I'm going with this? Now how am I supposed to know that fences won't hold up to a leaning Destroyer? Huumm? Anyway we accidentally broke the fence. Then I accidentally cut all round my eye trying to reach the greener grass like I was told too. I have decided Omar is an evil, lying Poofy poo head. I am in so much trouble now. From Dad and Uncle D for breaking the fence and from Mum for cutting my eye. Omar thinks its hilarious.

Mum made me work really hard last night (does she not know I'm poorly?) and I have a feeling the vet man is going to stick a needle in my bum later. Life is SO unfair.

PS. Where can I train to be a nurse? I want to stick needles in their bum and see how they like it!

PPS Does anyone know how to get sun cream off ones nose? I look like an ice-cream cone on legs.

19.06.2009

Dear Diary
I am exhausted. I am so tired I can hardly type . I fear for my life - I think Mum is trying to slim me into being a TB. I have been worked every day for over a WEEK! I need to come and stay with one of you nice people who will let me eat grass and not do anything. Mind you I have had fun this week!

Mum rode me all over the weekend which was great fun then Mum went away and Aunty Sarah rode me. Which is also fun but she's much bossier than Mum. She makes me actually work rather than just pretend to.

Then on Wednesday I sensed something was up. Dad washed my legs - now Dad never gives me a bath so I knew something was afoot. Mum arrived back and I was put on the lorry with fit mare. Wowee - thank you god! I had her all to myself for the journey there and back! More on that later.

When we arrived I realised we were back at a place I've been before so Mum got changed and we went into the warm up thing. Now I'm not keen on these places, the wind was banging and there were little ponies all over the place - I always worry about standing on one of them. But Mum kept telling me I was a good boy so we were ok. Then we went to the main ring and I saw the JUMPS!! Yippeee! Mum and I went round and I tried so hard for her but she pulled me up before one fence so I didn't get enough ooommmph and knocked it off. Poo! But she was pleased with me so that was cool.

Then Dad got on me. Now Mum has cobby legs and lots of bone so she doesn't really put a lot of pressure on with her legs. Dad does though so I thought he wanted me to go REALLY fast - apparently not from the telling off I got! Doh! We didn't do very well as I was going a bit too quick so Dad got off me and I stood and watched people for a while.

Then Dad got back on me and walked me round - I was a bit confused as I thought I'd finished but again apparently not. We went in and I swear the jumps were a bit higher? Crafty these humans. But I managed not to knock any off. What is the big deal? Its not hard? Mum was so pleased though and said we had to jump off. Jump off what? Can they not be clearer with these things?

I couldn't see anything to jump off then Dad took me back into the ring again and I KNEW there was nothing to jump off in there so I was very worried Mum might get mad with us. Then Dad seemed to forget the order of the jumps which I was a bit frustrated about because I think that's why we didn't win. I tried to make him jump them the way I'd remembered but he didn't want to. And he made me go faster and do really hard turns. I was rather confused - I got shouted at for going fast before? Anyway my legs were tired so I knocked a couple off but Mum and Dad seemed happy.

Fit mare then went off to do some jumping and I stood on the lorry. I then realised the greedy cow had eaten most of my hay!! humph! Mind you we did get hot and steamy on the way home - Mum said the camera steamed up so they couldn't see us.... oh yea baby........Mum couldn't see what we were REALLY up to. Which unfortunately was not a lot as she just talked about Poof bags all the way home. I tried breathing romantically into her ears but all it did was make her sneeze. I give up I really do. Maybe next time if Dad doesn't forget which way we're going and I find something to stand on to jump off then maybe she might Fancy me just a little bit? What do you think?

26.06.2009

Dear Diary

Sorry for being late today but I couldn't get to the laptop as Mum had it with her. I'm worried about Mum, really worried about her. I think she might have bumped her head – or maybe she's an alien and not Mum at all? But all of a sudden she's been making me go fast in the school! She never wants me to go fast but this last week before she went away that's all we did – trot, canter, trot, canter, trot, please-Mum-can-we-walk-I'm-pooped, canter, trot, canter. And on, and on, and on and on. What is wrong with the woman?

Even Uncle D said she's a changed woman – all confident. Not sure what that means but Uncle D asked if she was on drugs so maybe she's been taking confidence? How do I get her some help? What are the tell tale signs of confidence dependency? [Check me out! "Dependency" – sometimes I amaze even myself!]

She also has been trying to get me to go from walking to running – without trotting in between! How on earth am I supposed to do that? Everyone knows you have to do walk, trot THEN canter. This is what I mean I think she might have bumped her head because I swear she knew this before. I'm a tank not a Ferrari and whilst I like gong fast I do need to rev the engine first!

She also has become obsessed with circles. What's with the circles? Omar says she's going to have me drawing crop circles next – I don't know what this means but knowing my pooy headed Poof bags of an older brother it's probably not nice. She says we draw eggs not circles but I see no problem with this. Wasn't it only a few months back that the dizzy woman had us hunting for eggs? So she wants to make her mind up. Sheesh

Good news though – my cough has gone! Yippee. Mum got me this white stuff to put in my dinner and breakfast – which was great because it meant I got to get breakfast again since Dad has stopped the breakfast thing. Dad says it was my Columbian marching powder and Omar called me a smuck (or maybe smack?) head but I don't care – I am now better. If Mum doesn't kill me making me do endless transitions to canter I might get a chance to go out with fit mare again soon.

Mind you I'm not sure I want to go anywhere if Dad is going to ride me. Mum keeps joking that Dad will have to do some Godiva photos for charity – now I'm not sure what this is but I swear I heard Mum say Dad had to have no clothes on? What the HELL?! Is this some weird thing that all you forum perverts have come up with? I am not having my DAD on my back with no clothes on. Do I look like I swing that way? Huumm? Lord it's obscene. I am being sold into the porn industry. . If Omar and Dad want to do that sort of thing then that's up to them but keep me out of it. Anyway I swear Omar does swing that way so he'd probably be up for it. Luckily Dad doesn't seem to keen but if he comes near me with his flies so much as undone and I'm outta there. So Diary if I don't write next week – you know why………..

03.07.2009

Dear Diary
I fear this may be my last entry…….

I fear that by next week I will have completed slow roasting to death and will be sitting in between two pieces of bread on someone's table. Instead of someone saying excitedly "oh we're having meat loaf for dinner" instead it will be "we're having Hovis loaf".

Some time ago Uncle D had a birthday party and they sacrificed a pig over a fire. Well I think its someone else's birthday soon because I can empathise with that pig (I think I've spelt that big word wrong but my brain cells are like mush in a bucket). Its SO hot!

Needless to say this week has been rather quiet on the riding front - even Mum and Dad seem to realise someone had turned the heat up and its too hot to do anything. Mum rode me loads at the weekend but since she's been away Omar and I have just slow cooked.

Even fit mare, ginger-I'm-actually-quite-cute-for-a-ginge- mare have been wilting in the heat.

I have this morning organised a rain dance in the fields. Someone has to do something before we all die. We all have to run round once to the left, once to the right, rear up then buck. Apparently for it to truly work you have to sacrifice someone but no one seemed keen to volunteer. Personally I think that's just selfish. I couldn't even summon up the strength to help Mum clear out the trough yesterday although stealing her jug as we were halfway down the drive did seem to amuse her. She's rather easy to please is my Mum. Dad says its because she's simple - I'm not sure he'd say that when she can hear him though?!

The only other news is Mum has been bitten by horse flies more than me. How does that work? Surely I should get bitten by horse flies and Mum should be bitten by human flies? I am confused……….

10.07.2009

Dear Diary.
I nearly didn't write this week. I'm not sure there's any point. Last week I got all excited because someone on Horse and Hound online forum said I should be published. At last! Fame and fortune. I had visions of doing pony club rallies and signing autographs for fit little ponies who gaze adoringly at me….. of a stand at Burghley selling my book. But apparently Mum says I'm not good enough so I've got no chance of being famous. Its pants.

I'm not sure my Mum loves me anymore. First she says I'm not good enough at writing my Diary and then she threatens to sell me for a fiver. Timmy says that's like giving me away. I think some of it might be my fault. I think that I might just have pushed my luck a little too far at the beginning of this week.

It wasn't all my fault. Its just Omar and I were in a naughty mood and Mum is so easy to wind up. So it's not all me. Not that his royal highness Poof pants got any blame. Well to start off I know Mum now goes away on Sunday night so she comes to do us before she goes to the station. Now we thought we were doing her a favour. Last week she complained about how busy the train was so we thought we would help ensure no one wanted to sit next to her. Big mistake. Huge.
So firstly I got her trousers all mucky by refusing to come to the gate -she didn't seem too bothered so I went on with the plan. I pretended to be really thirsty so she went and fetched me a bucket of water, which I accidentally knocked all over her feet. Now she did say a few rude words but I thought it was because the water was cold. Apparently not.

When she brought the bucket back she held it for me so I took a big mouthful….. and spat it at her. This did NOT go down well so she took the bucket off me and offered it to Poof bags. So I signalled him by throwing my head collar at Mum, when she turned round to shout at me Poof bags stretched his neck really really high and then… spat water all over her head.

It was SO funny! She looked like a drowned rat. Dad was laughing too. Strangely Mum wasn't and her vocabulary suddenly grew really impressive and she used loads of words I've not heard before! Wow she's clever!

I think this might have been why she spent the rest of the time chuntering about selling me. Ooops. I'm not sure I want a new Mum. I mean the one I've got is a bit bonkers but I do love her.
Anyway yesterday I tried to make it up to her by being angelic in the school but I am very scared. She says because we're getting better we're going to have lessons with

a new man. Now Omar had a lesson with this man yesterday. He came back white and exhausted. He said it was the worst 1.5 hours of his life. Apparently this man was in the army and is really mean. I'm really scared. I'm not any good at getting down and giving anyone 50. I don't even know what it means. Diary help me!! Will I have to do star jumps?

24.07.2009

Dear Diary

I am sorry I didn't write last week but Mum was in Scotland and Dad was working away too so Aunty Vicky was looking after us. Aunty Vicky is cool as she makes great beds, gives us loads of food and best still doesn't make us do any work. But she hasn't got a computer I can borrow so I couldn't write.

So last week was fab, hanging out with my mates, ogling the girls, working on my mud pack and generally just dossing about. Then Mum came home and announced we've got to work hard as the army man is coming next week.

I've decided I might run away before this lesson from hell. The man sounds horrible. Mum has been making me do loads of trot, halt, walk, trot, halt, trot – yawn! But worst still she's come over all mean and if I don't go the instant she tells me she pulls me up and then asks me again by hitting me on the bum with the whip!! I am so offended! When did she get so bossy? She says that the army man won't be very impressed unless I try really hard and am very "off the leg". What does "off the leg" mean? I have four of them so which one am I supposed to be "off"? If I throw all four off the floor at once we'll fall over? I am so confused. Last weekend Uncle John and Aunty Mary came to visit. Now I don't think Aunty Mary likes me as I made her fall off – it was an accident but I thought it was funny. So this time Mum said Uncle John could ride me - he was cool, no control at all and he just let me whizz around the ménage really really fast – Mum was sort of laughing or maybe crying but I thought it was ace!

Yesterday Mum made me do loads of transitions and stuff again and then we went for a little walk up to the field. That was nice, Mum was being very brave and we went on our own. I like that as Mum talks to me loads and makes me feel very important. She is funny though. Today a big thing was flying low in the sky making load of noise, Mum kept telling me it was ok and stroking my neck – like I was scared of that thing? Seriously it was in the sky why would it worry me? Now nasty yellow things creeping up on us in the grass are scary but that thing – piff! No worries. Mum however obviously thinks I've been spending too much times with Poof bags and thought I'd run like a baby. Not a chance! I am a man not a mouse.

So what do you think I should do about army man? Seriously what with this "off the leg" stuff and the prospect of doing star jumps for an hour I am really wondering if doing a runner is the best option? Fit mare says he's nice but then he's a man and she probably spends the whole time looking at his bum – she is a long legged beauty but a total tart. So will one of you come and fetch me, let me stay at your pad just till he's gone? I'm seriously thinking being in the dog house might be more fun than being killed by some man treating me like I'm a squaddie? HELP!!

03.08.2009

Dear Diary
I am sorry that I didn't write on Friday – I was too exhausted to even put hoof to keyboard. It is only now, several days later than I am able to summon the energy to tell you about my horrific experience.

I am traumatised and quite possibly in need of therapy. I need massages from a bevy of fit mares just to be able to walk without it hurting. Any offers?!
Anyway as I told you all last week this was the week of the "army man". Well appearances can be quite deceptive – when he arrived he seemed rather nice, he gave me a pat, said he liked the look of me and seemed very harmless. In fact as Mum and I warmed up and he said he thought I was a cool dude I actually thought I could like the man. Mum got off me, he got on, he asked me to canter a few times, said I was lovely and got off. Great thought I – that's easy now I can go and eat some hay whilst Poof bags gets a work out. Oh no! How wrong was I? That was just for starters!

An HOUR and a HALF later I was dripping sweat, aching all over, being made to collect (what's wrong with full tilt GO!?), put my head in a poncy position, having to jump raised poles, normal poles then a jump! I seriously went off him when it started to rain and he didn't seem to think that meant it was time to stop. Mum was being all bossy and smacking me on the bum with a whip instead of letting me mooch along in walk, pulling me up when we cantered on the wrong leg and generally being a total teachers pet. Like she does that when he's not there!

The only saving grace was I didn't have to do any star jumps but seriously after an hour I'd have gratefully done them if that meant we were finished. I have a feeling he's saving them till next time. Yeah he might have said I was a seriously cool dude but he had better adjust his idea of what we do in lessons if he wants to be my friend. Crikey – I haven't sweat that hard since fit mare wriggled out of her rug in front of me last winter.

Omar had to be ridden by him this week too and he was NOT impressed. Army man made him jump and hack out on his own – Poof bags nearly pooed himself and they had a right argument in the car park. If army man wasn't so evil I might have found the image of Omar rearing up and throwing a totally ineffective hissy fit whilst army man held the reins in one hand and smoked a cigarette quite funny. Poof bags came back white and exhausted and NOT happy because army man said I have more stamina than him. I seriously wish he had said that in front of fit mare.

So all in all I am not happy and since he has been Mum has been a right bossy mare. If this is what its going to be like I might have to leave home. She went out today and "treated herself" to a pair of Springer spaniel stirrups to help her ride for longer. Humpf. How a dog helps matters I have no idea but no doubt this is a new dastardly idea from "GI Just No Fun".

Oh yeah will someone tell me what is wrong with being on the "wrong leg"? Eh? I have four of them and as long as I'm going forwards what does it matter which one is in front of the other one? God some people are just SO fussy.

10.08.2009

Dear Diary

I'm sorry I didn't write on Friday but Mum was down in London with the laptop so I couldn't use it. I have complained about this but Mum said she was busy trying to ensure I kept the lifestyle to which I have become accustomed. Not sure what that means but she had to go for an interview. Timmy says humans go for interviews with vampires but I think he's had too much sun recently.

Anyway this week has been quite good fun. Dad has been very busy too so I've not done a lot apart from help my friend Felix break fences and eat the greener grass on the other side. Omar did get us both in trouble the other day as he was supposed to be keeping guard but instead had stood staring manfully at the girls in the other field. As a result of that posing narcissi (my new word – d'ya like?) not paying any attention Felix and I got rumbled by his Mum. We were in trouble but Felix' Mum is less scary than mine so I'd rather it was her than my Mum that caught us. She just waves her arms at us and says she's mad. MAD? She wants to have lessons from my Mum on how to act when you're mad. Felix's Mum just looks funny and we ignore her. Even big old Felix would rather have his man bits removed again than upset my Mum.

On Thursday Mum told me Monty was going to come and ride me. This worried me immensely. Monty lives three stables down and I have always suspected may go both ways. I was not looking forward to this experience at all. I also know I'm a big strong boy but why did I have to carry him? He's got 4 legs of his own. Fortunately it appears Mum has a friend called Monty (phew), so he took me and Dad took Poof bags and we went for an all male hack to the woods. It was fun because like Uncle John, Uncle Monty has got no control, is very brave and likes going fast. The bad news was it was rainy and the woods were very muddy…. and Uncle Monty didn't seem to know the "we aren't supposed to jump in puddles rule"….. well like I was going to tell him! Mum didn't look too amused at the state I came back in but I had fun! I think a bit of mud makes me look less girlie and much more manly. Mum says I look like a bog trotter.

Mum then has ridden me all weekend with those new Springer spaniel stirrups. I want to lodge a formal complaint to which ever idiot designed those things. Before Mum only did about 30-40 minutes on me because her leg hurt. NOW she does forever on me and only seems to notice how long we've been working for when I start acting as though I am about to die. I was so sweaty today it was running off my legs. The woman is like evil^2 (d'ya like that? Clever for a hairy boy aren't I?!!) with these things on. She did give me a cold shower afterwards but even so I think they are an evil invention.

Apparently Army man is coming again this week so we are building up our fitness. OUR fitness? All she does is sit there, bash me on the bum with a whip and make me go in circles. How is that hard work for her? Lord you humans have no idea at all. Try running a dressage test and see how you like it! Anyway I have the next 3 days off then "GI Just No Fun" is back. I can't blinking wait……

14.08.2009

Dear Diary

How do I go about divorcing my parents? I want a new set. Ones that give those mints with the holes in them, cuddle me lovingly and DON'T make me have lessons with Evil Army Man.

This week had been fun, Mum rode me loads at the weekend which was great although tiring now she has those dratted spaniel stirrups! Then Aunty Vicky looked after us during the week, fed us lots of tea, made us really comfy big beds to sleep in (that's another thing why can't Mum and Dad make beds like Aunty Vicky?) and didn't make me do any work. Fab! Poof bags and I have been chilling out, eating grass, watching the flirty ladies and generally enjoying life.

Until yesterday. When HE came.

Poof bags went first which was fine by me as I stayed inside and ate hay. 1.5 HOURS later he came back. Exhausted, defeated and drenched – since it wasn't raining I had to assume it was with sweat – SO not a good look, even on him.

I did try to avoid having to go and be beasted by refusing to open my mouth to put my bridle on but apparently Mum has seen that little trick before and before I could clench my molars she'd got that horrible bit of metal in my mouth.

Then it started, the "off the leg", "correct canter lead", collected trot, no napping, no slowing down and no catching my breath, session from HELL. He made Mum make me jump over this grid thing, which in fairness was quite good fun, then he made us go in the jumping paddock. Mum hates it in there as apparently I am a knat on grass? At least that's what I think she told him – Timmy who was hanging over the fence and making unhelpful comments, said it sounded more like she said "tw" not "kn" at the front but he's old and I swear his hearing is going. He also said that when I jump over a fence my bum looks so big it blocks out the sun. He made be old and wise but seriously he makes comments like that again I am so going to bite his moustache.

So we did another looooonnnnggg session in the paddock with him making Mum jump – judging from the way she was breathing I don't think she enjoyed that much but heh this was her stupid idea. THEN, then he made me go all the way up to the big field and made Mum walk to catch him up, turn me round trot off 100 m, turn round and catch him back up again. Now I'm sorry but if I walk too quick for him either bring his own horse or don't bother. Why should I have to keep turning round and doing twice the distance I need to? THEN, then he made Mum turn round and go back home the way we had come on our own. By this stage I have to be honest I was that pooped that a small tiger could have jumped out of a bush and I wouldn't have cared. The man is Satan.

Apparently he was very pleased with Poof bags and me. Ha! Tell it to two horses who care! Mum and Dad have booked him AGAIN for 2 weeks time. Poof bags and I did bond over the situation though – we are plotting how we get shot of this bloke quick sharp. All this working and being made to do things properly is so not fun.

Anyway I swear I heard Mum say she's taking me out jumping tonight – I seriously hope not. My legs are so tired I can't do a trotting pole let alone jumps. Where has the easy going, fun loving Mum gone? This new mean version I'm going off rapidly.

So a) does anyone know any hitman horses that can bump this bloke off for us for a carrot and a gob full of pasture mix (I'd offer more but I'm wasting away as it is)? And b) how do I divorce my parents – anyone know any solly ickitors (that's what Timmy says we need) who will work for half a haynet and some spat out calm and condition?

Please help, hope is fading and my legs can't deal with much more of this………..

22.08.2009

Dear Diary
I have a dilemma. A big one. I have decided I love my Mum more than anything in the world, but I don't think she loves me at the moment.

Last week after Evil Army Man had been, Mum announced she was going to be brave and we were going out jumping. I was tempted to point out there's nothing brave about sitting on top of me, pointing me at a fence, swearing a few times and then shutting her eyes whilst I do all the work. Tempted but not brave enough to say it………..

Anyway I was loaded up and off we went to a new place. It was ok, the warm up thing was very big which I prefer and the jumps were ok. We had a bit of a problem at one of the jumps, if truth be told Mum wobbled as we landed so I thought she wanted me to go right, I then saw Dad so cantered over to say hi. Note to self – must not do this in the middle of a round of jumps. We went back jumped the jump and carried on but I was tired and we hit the last jump. Mum was pleased though so that was cool.

Then on Saturday – well I couldn't believe it! Mum rode me out with fit mare, Poof bags, lanky legs boy and wise Mont. Wise Monty is as old as Timmy which means they are old   like dinosaurs. Mum NEVER rides me out like this so I think she's been taking that confidence stuff again. It was FAB. We went down to the woods and rode for miles. The only down side was Mums singing. I love her but seriously I've heard cats yowling sound more tuneful. Even Monty who is old and so deaf was wincing (well either that or he had something in his eye).

THEN on Sunday Mum took me on my own round the big field. What is wrong with the woman? She NEVER does these things. WOW! The singing is getting a tad annoying though as she doesn't seem to know many songs and those she does know she murders. I know this because we have a radio in the stables so we listen to tunes man. Fi's Mum leaves it on radio 2 but as soon as they've gone we tune it to some banging drum and bass and a bit of R&B. I tell you the moves fit mare can pull to Fifty Cent are enough to give a boy a heart attack.

Best of all when we got back she gave me a lovely groom, gave me some carrots and a big tub of lickit! YUM YUM YUM.

Now if I'm honest that's when the week went down hill. I love my lickit and as I was tired decided the best thing was to take it out of the silly tub Mum puts it in and lie down with it to eat it. Unfortunately I fell asleep and managed to roll on it. Now I'm failing to see why it being all over me is a problem..............? Honestly the fuss Mum made was SO out of proportion. It gave me lots of opportunity to ask if anyone wanted a lick of my molasses covered body........... Unfortunately the only person who said yes was Felix and THAT wasn't going to happen in my lifetime.

Now admittedly several days later it is still stuck in my feathers and I'm not sure how Mums going to get it off but she's clever – I'm sure she'll think of something.

So not sure what I'm doing this weekend – Mum has mentioned going to a car wash but I am baffled as to what this has to do with me?

We're also going to the pub on Sunday. We're all riding there apparently. Timmy says the pub is like the dog house only where human men go to avoid their wives. Should be interesting then......

28.08.2009

Dear Diary
My name is Hovis, I am 6 years old and I like drinking beer.

It's all Mums fault, she took me to that pub place last weekend and I've found out how nice the stuff they drink there is. Last Sunday fit mare, nutty Alf, Poof bags, wise Monty, looney legs, mature-but-fit Fi, scary mare and I rode out of the yard together which was VERY exciting. I've never been out in a group that big before. I did get so excited I jogged a bit but Mum shouted at me so I stopped. We rode for a long way which was fine except nutty Alf did the whole thing sideways. He freaks me out to be honest, he looks loads like Poof bags but he's all white where Poof bags is all dark. And he's MENTAL! I don't think Mum likes him too much either so we tried to keep out of his way.

Then finally we arrived at this house which had loads of seats outside and we rode across this funny stone stuff which made a really loud noise when you stood on it. Poof bags and co were having a duck fit over it but I thought it was kind of cool. Then Mum and all the other people got off and took us into this garden place where they let us eat the grass! All these other people arrived and were cuddling me and saying how handsome I was – ha! They didn't say anything to Poof bags so he was most put out. Mum and Dad and the others then all had a drink of this nice smelling stuff in big glasses. When Mum wasn't looking I stuck my nose in her glass and YUM I like that stuff! Mum said I wasn't allowed anymore as I was underage – why do you have to be old to drink nice things? It's so unfair.

Then after Mum and everyone had eaten some funny smelling bread things we mounted up and rode all the way home. It was good fun! Mum said I was brilliant apart from the point near to home when Alf ran past me and I thought "what the heck" and ran after him. Apparently Mum hauling on my bit and shouting things like "whoa you big fat person-of-unknown-parentage" meant she wanted me to stop. I wish she'd be clearer on these things.

Mum let me have the day off on Monday which was nice of her until I realised she wanted to give me a bath. She used this stuff called fairy which has really ruined my cred on the yard. Seriously is the woman hell bent on having people thinking I prefer Poof bags to fit mare? I am NOT a fairy. Why can't I have shampoo called – macho man or something? Anyway I give Mum her due she's got my feathers very clean. Apparently all this bathing and mane tidying is because we're going "showing" on Sunday. What's "showing"? It sounds a bit poncy to be honest and I am getting a little worried. Last night Aunty L plaited my tail to show Mum and I looked a right idiot! Mum says we have to trot round whilst some person decides who's the best looking. Old Timmy said it sounds like Mums taking me to a beauty pageant and I will also have to show a "talent". I'm not sure I've got one of those so how do I show it? The only thing I can think of is showing how to eat a lickit in under 3 minutes – will that do? Any other ideas?

Anyway I have to go soon – HE is coming later so I'm going to find a tree to try to hide behind before Mum can find me. I do not want to be beasted by commando bossy boots today, I'm still traumatised by the tail plaiting. Right, I'm off….. I wonder if I lie down really flat in the field Mum might think I'm too exhausted to be worked? Hum………..

29.08.2009

Dear Diary
Just to let you all know I survived the army man. Seriously if he wasn't such a bossy man I could quite like the dude. He says nice things about me but then makes me work my feathers off.

He also suggested that I'd lost some weight - "yes!" I thought he's going to tell Mum I need more food. Alas no the cheeky bu**er told Mum I looked good now I have lost some "podge". PODGE? EXCUSE ME?! I am a highly tuned, well muscled man mountain, I have no room on my toned body for PODGE! That was merely storage of fat in case of desperate times.

At this point I did decide I could go off the man quite quickly.

I think Mum has gone off him too as I swear she suggested he didn't know who his Dad was on several occasions. This seemed to coincide with the times he put the jumps up even higher but I might be mistaken.

Once again by the end I was sweating more than if fit mare had suggested a twosome in the hay barn and breathing harder than I ever have when I've watched her get ready for bed (not that I watch her you understand - that would be pervy - just sometimes I have *accidentally* being looking in that direction at the same time as she's putting her pjs on........)

From the way Mum was puffing I think she might have been pooped too. I have to question Mums brain - why does she PAY this man to put us both through this? Spending the money on lickits would be a far far better idea. Could one of you suggest that please?

Oh and note to self - standing in the middle of the field not looking at your Mum so you can't see her apparently doesn't mean she can't see you. And pretending to be suddenly deaf doesn't get you out of army PT either. Damn it!

01.09.2009

Dear Diary
I will keep this short but in summary I'm not sure I like this showing thing...........
Mum gave me a bath on Saturday and really scrubbed me, I'll give her her due she got me very very clean!

She then trussed me up like a turkey with leg warmers on. Timmy said I look like an extra from Fame. I'm not sure what that was but even I thought I looked stupid. There are times when a boy could seriously dislike his mother.

Then on Sunday morning she rudely got me out of bed and started grooming AGAIN. Aunty L plaited my tail like a girl then I was unceremoniously dragged onto the lorry and told under no circumstances was I to rub, poo or wee on myself. Seriously do they have any idea what its like to be back there when Dad is driving? They'd poo themselves I can tell you.

Anyway we got there and Mum and Aunty Sarah got me off the lorry and undid my leg warmers to reveal gleaming white feathers - THEN they covered me in baby powder! I smelt like a babies bum - I was SO embarrassed I wanted to die (particularly as there was a foxy mare in the trailer next door). So there am I with my tail tied up like a girl, smelling like a baby and wafting talc every time I moved. Seriously the chances of me pulling were close to zero.

Mum was talked into doing some "in hand" thing which basically meant I had to run around with Mum whilst some old woman told her I "lacked impulsion". I would have shown her impulsion if Mum hadn't stopped me from kicking the old bat. Mum only went in the silly class so the other bloke in it had someone to beat. He was an 18HH Shire who made me look like a Shetland! He was HUGE! Plus he did it at county shows so I can live with being beaten by him. Besides which I didn't Fancy my chances if he got mad at me! I got a rosette though which was cool.

Then Mum took me away from the old crow and put my saddle on and we went for a little ride in front of a nice lady who said I was lovely. Apparently Mum needs to relax more and "allow my lovely paces to be seen" - I tell Mum this all the time but does she listen to me?!

Once again we got beaten by the big man but heh he was rather good. I got a bit carried away with my cantering and Mum took half the arena to stop me so I think fair doos he was better. The nice lady said I was young though and the big man was much older than me so he'd had more practise. I liked her and didn't try to kill her when she gave Mum her rosette.

Mum was pleased with me and said I'd been a really good boy so that was cool and I got loads of treats. I'm not sure it made up for me smelling like a babies bum but it at least made me feel better.

I'm not sure how much of this showing lark Mum wants to do and I much prefer jumping over things. The second lady was very nice but the one who made me run round and said rude things about me wasn't. Next time I'm going to tread on the old bags toe. That's of course if there is a next time.............

04.09.2009

Dear Diary
I think I might be in trouble again. This time I'm not sure its entirely my fault but still I have to shoulder the blame. Life is, at times, so unfair.

As you will know from my show report last week Mum and I went showing last weekend. I behaved, didn't kick the judge who was rude about me and Mum was pleased. So far so good......

On Monday Mum gave me the day off and fed me carrots = ace day.

On Tuesday Mum took me for a little ride on my own and we had a nice time round the field. Then on the way back there was a very large Chandlers gas lorry coming down our drive. The driver was nice and stopped but the drive is very very narrow so to get past it I literally could feel it against my whiskers - with an electric fence at the other side of me.

I wasn't too sure but Mum stoked my neck and said it would be ok, so keeping a wary eye on the beast I walked past it. Everyone who saw it said their horses wouldn't have gone past so I was rather chuffed with myself.

Then came the oooops point of the week.

Aunty Sarah has a friend who is having a bad time at the moment. To cheer her up Aunty Sarah decided to take her for a ride and borrowed me to take her friend. So fit mare and I went stubble field racing! Yeeehaaaaa! It was ACE fun! We went so fast! For miles! Man that girl has long legs and I had to work hard to keep up. Alas my recently snow white feathers didn't survive this encounter and did not return white. Aunty Sarah said Mum would be mad about me being in stubble fields so we weren't allowed to tell her. Three guesses who told her? That's right - Poofus bagus of the big gob. Mum was not amused.

To make things worse Poofy is telling me he's going to Burghley on Saturday to meet his adoring fans. I didn't think you lot liked him? Anyway Mum says its only a sponsored ride and I'm not allowed to go in case I get too strong and tank off with her. She has said I can go next year but I am well miffed. Fit mare is going with him too - its so not fair.

Omar says I'm not allowed to go because Burghley is a posh place and I'm a bog trotting commoner. That's not true is it?

Anyway if any of you are going and see a very good looking [grudgingly though I admit that] Poof having apoplexy over everything - that'll be my brother. Kick him for me!

07.09.2009

Dear Diary
This weekend I lost my confidant, my mentor and my friend. Wise Timmy died in his field in my Dads arms on Saturday morning. Aunty Sarah and Mum were with him too and the sun had even come out to say goodbye.

The yard has lost its patriarch and we'll all be the worse off for his passing.

You'll be missed wise old man:
Missed by the hundreds of children you taught to ride
Missed for the way your moustache would wiffle over the top of the bars as you snaffled my hay
Missed for the times you and I were in the arena together and played chicken together - two big Clyde's thundering towards each other
Missed for the way you were allowed to roam the yard untethered to nick the apples off the tree
Missed for the way you'd canter rings round the unsuspecting who'd be told to fetch "old" Timmy from the field.
Missed for the way you sometimes forgot you were supposed to be old and sensible and would buck riders off
Missed for the way every Sunday you'd lie in the field stretched out with Charlie in the sunshine
Missed for your wiseness, your softness and for your ability to make anyone who met you smile
Missed more than anything for simply being you.

It appears God wanted one of his equine angels back with him, but Tim if I can give a 10th of the happiness in my lifetime that you gave in yours I will be a happy horse.

Goodnight wise old friend, sleep well and when my time comes wait with Bertie at the gate for me.

11.09.2009

Dear Diary
I have a new career. Apparently I am about to get a suit and a job in the city – Monty tells me that's what people who are total bankers do. I know I am a good banker because Mum has spent most of this week telling me so – she's SO insightful is my Mum.

As you'll know from my entry on Monday we lost dear old Timmy at the weekend so everyone started the week quite subdued. Aunty Sarah took me out for a ride on Monday which I thought was cool – until I realised we were test driving a new bit. Pants! Apparently someone has told Mum that whilst the Pelham she had me in is ok I'm still leaning on her hands. Damn right I am!! Do you know how heavy my head is? Mum is a big strong girl – she can hold me up when I get tired – after all all she's done is sit on me whilst I got tired!

Anyway I found out later this week who's daft idea that was – but more on that in a moment. Mum rode me on Tuesday and Wednesday and that's when she told me that I'm destined for a career in the city. "You great big banker" she shouted several times. She told me quite a lot so I think this means she's very impressed!

Impressed is not what I was yesterday. Depressed more like. HE came. Evil Army Man who I swear is trying to turn me into Combat Clydesdale. Apparently this new bit was his idea – I should have guessed – I swear the man sits all day trying to figure out new ways to ruin my fun. He brought his girlfriend with him yesterday; she is in foal and is a very nice lady. She said I was handsome, cool, charming, sexy, beautiful, smart....... ok maybe she didn't say ALL those things but I'm sure she was thinking them. She liked me more than Poof bags so she can come again.

Under her influence even GI Just No Fun said I was cool and was nice about me too – "aha!" I thought "He's coming round" – then he ruined it by suggesting I would look great pulling a cart. Now there was just no need for comments like that. Ok my ancestors pulled carts, I admit that, but his ancestors swung in trees and picked fleas out of each others hair. Do you see me mentioning that?! Hum?

Anyway yesterday we spent doing circles. CIRCLES? What happened to jumping? Apparently Mum hasn't been well all week but since she just sits there, points me at the jump and shuts her eyes, I fail to see what that had to do with anything? And why does she need to be able to turn me in small circles in canter? At what point hurtling around a jumping course like an unstoppable force of nature do we need to be able to do pretty circles? I wish Mum would stop bathing me in funny smelling shampoos –I swear its making people think I should be treated like a big girl.

To make matters worse Poof bags and fit mare went off together in the lorry and he told me later GI Jo had taken them to the cross country course. Life is SO unfair!! I LOVE XC! It's my forte (d'ya like my big words?!). Poofy is the dressage circle queen and I am the Destroyer the XC machine. He wets himself if he sees a stick in the road – these delicate types are not meant to be allowed onto cross country courses – that should be left to real men......like me!

To make things even more depressing Fit mare is well into Poof bags at the minute and has taken to calling out to him all the time. Life sucks. We have got a date this afternoon but I swear if she mentions that dark brooding plank of a brother of mine even once I'm so going to bite her scrumptious bum............

28.09.2009

Dear Diary

I'm back!!

Mum has been away seeing my grandparents and the beastly woman didn't leave the laptop for me to keep you up to date.

Much has happened since my last entry so I will attempt to fill you in.

As you may recall I was last going out for a romantic walk with fit mare. Well that kind of was a disaster...... I fell over. Completely over my own feet and ended up in a bit of a heap. Mum was livid and fit mare I fear now thinks I am too much of an idiot to be seen in public with her ever again. I admit to it being my fault – I was keeping a wary eye on road work signage to protect Mum from any evil lurking behind it and didn't see the hole in the ground. It was so embarrassing!

After that Mum gave me a day off and called nice Aunty Claire to come and have a look at my back. She gave me a nice massage, said there was nothing wrong with me and refused to give me a sick note. Fit mare got 2 days off! How is that fair? Mind you Aunty Sarah then rode me whilst Mum was away so we got to go very very fast across the fields. Which is ALWAYS cool!

Then Mum introduced me to a new man who's going to do our shoes. He's so trendy! I like him. He has the coolest whiskers I have ever seen. They're like the sheepskin blinkers posh SJ mare wears. I wonder if he looks about when jumping over fences? I SO wish Mum would let me grow mine like his – she shaves mine off.

New shoe man did Poof bags feet and fit mares feet and then said he couldn't do mine. Apparently he needed to make me some shoes specially. Poof bags said this is because I'm a special child and need dustbin lids instead of shoes. I prefer to think that it means I am a big macho beast who needs big macho shoes. Anyway he had to come back specially with my shoes later that week. He does keep referring to my weight which I think is a little personal and is the cause of my latest embarrassment (which I will come to in a minute) so we could fall out but I'm on the side of liking him at the minute.

Which brings me to my next point. Over reach boots. They are from the same satanistic, ruin-a-boys-standing-in-the-neighbourhood school of thinking as spaniel stirrups and lemon smelling shampoo. I'm sorry but what the heck are they about? Apparently my feet are a bit poorly so new shoes man has fitted my dancing shoes differently. Because of this I have to wear these idiotic things on my feet for the next

6 weeks. I look an utter plank. I look like a hairy spanner on legs. The wreckage of my street cred can be found down the lane in case anyone wonders what it is. I look like I'm wearing some random pony's trainers around my ankles. I am doomed to be single for the rest of my life, if its not fly masks it's over reach boots…

Finally whilst Mum was away army man came round. You may note I've not called him "evil" this week. That's because finally I think he's coming round to my way of thinking. Because Mum was away Dad had a lesson on Poofy and then a lesson on me. Finally army man got to see the Destroyer in full flow! He was impressed (I could tell!) and said a few nice things about me. If we can just get to see eye to eye on the amount of work I have to do then I could even like the man. He does think I can jump a little bit. You see ladies I might be a big feathery beast but inside is a Milton just waiting to come out……..(come out of where we'll discuss next week!!)

02.10.2009

Dear Diary
Yesterday I had the fright of my life. Maybe-not-so-Evil Army Man came, but this time it was different…………. For a start we were all in the stables (me, Poof bags and fit mare) and Mum and Dad weren't dressed for riding. Most odd I thought. Then he produced a bucket full of torture implements!! OMG!! I instantly took back any bad things I have ever said about him, shut my eyes and prayed to the patron saint of "save my big hairy arse" as hard as I could.

Upon opening my eyes I saw that he was doing fit mares teeth! Phew! Lord she did make a fuss though. I love and lust after her with all my heart but lord that girl is high maintenance! Mind you Poof bags wasn't much better – it must be something to do with their good breeding. Apparently Mum has traced Poof bags fathers side back for 5 generations and he has amazing blood lines. I did wonder what mine would show but apparently you can't trace the blood lines if your Mum wasn't fussy.

Mind you Poofy has had the smirk wiped of his face by Cool New Shoes Man. He came to see us again this week and Poofy has had to have special shoes made too. Ha!! Not laughing now are you TB face?!! Humm? Ok I have to have special shoes too but that's besides the point (see my update earlier this week). My teeth were fine – I could have told them that. Mum doesn't let me have sweets or anything so how could I have bad teeth? Whilst doing my teeth not-so-evil-army man was very nice about me – apparently he is amazed by my athleticism and how good I am at jumping for a big boy. I was rather flattered till I wondered if this was a cunning plan? Say nice things about me then work me even harder? Humm? He did tell Mum she'd have to be braver as I was being "wasted" – yeah too right mate I'm wasting away. Tell Mum to feed me more instead of waffling about how high off the floor I can jump.

Mum has being riding me all week and I think to be honest some days she does get out of bed and leave her brain at home. Some days she has ridden very well and she has been pleased with me, then other days she's ridden like a big booby and she's not pleased with me. Eh? How does that work? Fit mare told me I have to accept Mum is a woman and thus always right but I'm not sure about that? If Mum is always right why is she making me wear over reach boots which are definitely not right by anyone's standards? Why does she wash me in girlie shampoo and make me wear girlie coloured rugs? I think being a man stinks sometimes………..

16.10.2009

Dear Diary
Wow what an exciting weekend I had last week!

I went HUNTING!! Whoop whoop!

It started with Mum giving me a really good groom, then Aunty Sarah putting my travel boots on. This confused me when I saw Poofy had also got his travel boots on. I was glad to see that he looks as silly as I do with the silly things on but we never go anywhere together so I did start to worry Mum had finally sold us as a job lot…

Anyway after Poof bags took aaaaggggeees to get on the lorry Mum loaded me and off we went. We still had no idea where we were off to so I entertained myself by trying to pull Poof bags whiskers out through the bars of the lorry. He kept moving though which is so not the point of the game.

Mum wasn't in the lorry which confused us but occasionally as we went round roundabouts I could see her in the car behind us. Most odd.

We eventually got to a big field and Mum and Aunty Sarah got me ready whilst Dad sorted out Poofy. I couldn't see any jumps or anything but there was quite a few other horses there. It was all very strange. Then we heard this odd noise. It sounded like the one who barks but lots of them and they kept howling like the wind does though the stables sometimes.

Then all of a sudden there were dog things everywhere and we set off behind them. Aunty Sarah was riding me and Mum set off in the car again. I didn't understand what the heck was going on but we went on a lovely hack with all these other horses and of course the dog things. It was a nice hack and we got to jump some nice big logs and things. Then when we got to a field the dogs started acting really strangely and running about barking and things. Then we were off!! I saw Mum flash by as we ran past, following the dogs and these bossy men on the horses at the front. It was fab!! Poof and I ran like the wind, following all the others. I hadn't got a clue what we were doing but it was great fun and dead fast!! Wooohhhaaaaaa!! Then the dogs seemed to find what they were after – which to my disappointment was just a bloke in a jumper. What did he have that they wanted so bad we had to run fast to catch up with him? Anyway then we had another nice hack and got back to where we started. Mum was there and she seemed very pleased with Poof bags and I so lord knows what we were supposed to have done.

We got home and Mum gave me a nice bath, lots of nice food and lots of cuddles. Mum is one odd woman sometimes.

She's been away for most of this week but came back last night to ride me. We had a fun time although she is getting rather fixated with me doing perfect circles and holding my head just so. I was ignoring that bit so Dad got on to show her the lessons he's been having with Aunty Cathy. Aunt Cathy is really cool and a very good rider but a boy could go off her pretty quick if she's going to start teaching Mum and Dad how to make me hold my head like some sort of dressage queen. I am the Destroyer – not a dainty pansy who ponces round in circles. Hummpphhff. Anyway I'm kind of hoping we get to go on another hack with the dogs soon and that Mum soon forgets about this dressage poop. I wonder how I can convince her that I am far too manly to do it? Ideas on a postcard please?!!!

23.10.2009

Dear Diary

This week I have decided that my brother is a girl. He may be all big, dark, brooding and sexy on the surface but actually he is a girl.

Last Friday Cool New Shoes Man visited and made sure that my shoes were on tight. I didn't like to tell Mum but I had stood on my own feet in the field so that's why my shoes were loose. I was hoping that he'd say I didn't have to wear my silly over reach boots anymore but alas no.

On Saturday Mum and Dad, Poofy and I went on a nice little hack round the woods then we went in the school. I decided that I couldn't be bothered to mis-behave so I was really good and Mum let me jump over a jump that was up!! Weeeehhhaaa! THEN on Sunday we went on another long hack with those dogs that appear to keep losing things!! I only said in last weeks Diary I wanted to go again so I'm starting to think Mum reads this!! Maybe I should start writing about more food and a girlfriend? Anyway we were at a different place this week so I'm not sure how they'd lost the man in the red jumper again but hey hum its fun helping them find him. There were more people there this week and Poofy didn't like it. Another horse went bananas and Poof bags floored Dad. Ohh SO not a good move. We were then made to go home in disgrace. Lord my older brother is thick. Seriously if he doesn't start to grow a set of cahones soon I'm going to buy him a skirt for Christmas.

So my hack with the doggies was shorter than I'd wanted. Needless to say I was an angel – I know what side my bread is buttered on! Ha just because I'm all big and hairy don't mean this boy is dense – oh no!

Mum then went away to work and came back on Weds. Yesterday HE came. Army man. Note the lack of "evil" these days – this is because I really think he has come around to my way of thinking. He did worry me a bit when he nuzzled my nose though – I want him to like me but not THAT much! Come on man – we're men. High five me or something but please don't make it look like you're kissing me – I have a reputation to uphold you know what I'm saying? He also seems to be trying to grow a fluffy nose band, like the cool shoes man has fluffy blinkers. They both must gawp about or look at the floor whilst jumping – well it's the only thing I can think of?

So yesterday we did LOADS of jumping, in canter!! Yippppeee!! Army man says Mum has to be brave and trust me – like duuh? What have I been saying for ages? Just sit still, don't interfere and let me get on with it! It was great fun though even if I was pooped by the time we'd finished. I'd not sweat that much since fit mare did a runner last week in her nightie. Phew mama – those long legs, an early morning dew and her still in her night clothes – I've come over all peculiar just thinking about it!!

She's hurt her leg so hasn't been allowed to come out and play – I did offer to give her a massage but I think she's also hurt her ears because she didn't seem to hear me? Anyway Army Man and Mum were very pleased with me so it was a good day. Now if my suspicion is right and Mum is reading this......... how about a bit more tea, breakfast and half an hour in fit mares stable please ma?!!!!!!!!!!!!

06.11.2009

Dear Diary

It has been an awful week. The love of my life is in horsepital. She has been kicked and now has a poorly leg. Mum has told me she's going to be ok but I am very worried about her. I'm thinking of sending her a gift in horsepital – do you think a swede says I care or that I don't get much pocket money? I'm not sure if I can stretch to a lickit unless anyone knows where I can get a discount version? Anyway hopefully she will be home soon so I can gaze adoringly at her but in the meantime I will think about how to show her I care.

Anyway apologies for not writing last week – Mum was in France so she'd taken the laptop with her.

Last week was a bit quiet as Mum was away but we had a nice ride at the weekend. This week Aunty Sarah has taken me out with Poofy a couple of times which is fun. I love Mum dearly but Aunty Sarah likes to go fast!

Last week we moved into a new field so I helped Mum and Dad clean out the water trough. It appears that the mice in the area must be depressed because quite a few had committed suicide in the trough. Yuk! Mum and Dad did not seem to appreciate my help in cleaning the trough out though – honestly some people are so ungrateful. Mum is in despair as the gateway to the new field is very muddy and so my feathers are a tad dirty. Ok – for a tad dirty read "absolutely filthy". I am actually going to try to roll in the mud today because later HE is coming.

As I told you last time Army Man came I'm warming to him more all the time but I am getting worried he might like me in all the wrong ways. After last time him nuzzling me I thought if I get all dirty he may be put off doing this and at least give me a manly high five instead? I'm not looking forward to having to work hard though even if it is fun jumping – do you think if I get dirty enough and lie down I'll be disguised like a lizard?

New shoes man is coming later too – apparently he's made me some cool new big boys shoes which I'm hoping will mean I can stop wearing these daft over reach boot things. A boy can hope can't he?

Anyway must go and try to hide before Mum gets back – any suggestions of where a 16.2HH big boy like me can hide in a field?

13.11.2009

Dear Diary

This week has not been a good one. As I wrote last week I was trying to hide from army man and Mum alas (as you all told me would happen) they found me and thus I had to do some work. This week Evil Army Man (yes he is evil again – I'll explain why in a minute) made Mum and I do a single jump a few times then put up what he called a "double". Now this is where the evil bit has crept in again.

I am a 16.2HH BIG boy and whilst I may be a bit dim I KNEW that there was not enough room between the first jump and the second jump to land my big manly legs, stride then hurtle my body over the next bit. Seriously the man needs his eye sight testing. So in order to help Mum I cleverly saved us by ducking out the side between the two jumps – see I am not stupid!!

Alas evil man seemed to spot my cunning tactic and so did something about it, something I didn't see till the last minute. Mum and I came at the jump in canter; I jumped the first bit, twisted athletically in mid air to duck out and WHOA!! POLE! Where the blazes did that come from? I heroically tried to jump it to save us both but then Mum let the side down and fell off. Seriously how are we supposed to run away to fight another day if the daft woman dismounts me mid air?

The good side to this little issue was army man then took the second part down and I happily proved that if he's reasonable I can jump anything. This "double" malarkey is surely only for you skinny TB types not us big butch men?

Anyway the rest of the week has not been too good either. Cool New Shoes Man came on Friday and put me some more big boys shoes on thankfully this time with a toe clip so I'm hoping that's the end of the very unmanly over reach boot incident....

My poor darling fit mare is still in horsepital and has had to have another operation. The poor darling girl. I am just hoping they have not scarred those wonderful legs of hers. We are all hoping she will be back soon but a boy misses watching her get dressed in the morning even if I swear the little strip tease is more for Poof bags than me.

Then to cap it all off I am ill too.

Mum thought I seemed a bit "off" – does that mean she thought I smelt? - so asked the vets to come. Apparently I have a good heart and lungs and my temperature is normal. Now all I will say on that subject is that if that man vet EVER does what he did to me that day again I will plant him through the back stable wall! The insult! Really.

Anyway he also took some blood from me - which I would like back please - and then rang Dad with the results the next day.

I apparently have a very low white and red blood cell count. I'm not really sure what that means but the vet man came back yesterday and gave me two injections and apparently Dad has to give me some more. I don't mind injections but one of them was HUGE!! I know I'm a big boy but I'm not sure there was any need for that.

So all in all it's been a pants week, Mum is moaning about her neck, fit mare is still in horsepital and I'm poorly too. I need comforting, I need food parcels, I need a massage, I need........... well any offers ladies?!

20.11.2009

Dear Diary

I am sorry for writing late today but I have been awaiting news of my beloved. She has been very very poorly in horsepital and Mum had told me that I should be very worried about her.

Today the much awaited news has come that hooves crossed she is on the mend. Mum said she's not out of the woods yet but she is a bit better. This confused me immensely - I thought she has hurt her leg so not sure which woods she's been out in? I hope she's not pulled anyone else whilst at horsepital. Here am I sick with worry and she's on the pull? That had better not be the case or the treats I had saved up for her upon her return will go to someone else instead.

Mum has told me that the vibes of the horse and hound online community should not be underestimated... so I was wondering can you all send me some vibes that when my gorgeous leggy babe comes back that she'll Fancy me and not Poof bags? Pleeeeaaase?

Anyway in other news I am still ill. Ladies I am a shadow of my former self. So till fit mare comes back does anyone Fancy playing Florence nightinmare? The vet is apparently coming back soon to take more of my blood – what's with that? Monty said now I am famous perhaps they are using my blood to try to clone me? Poof bags pointed out that God broke the mould when he made me - I was most touched until he explained that God would rather hell freeze over than there be two of me around.

Anyway Mum has said I can have more food and I don't have to do any work till next week so maybe this illness has its upsides.

Anyway can I have some get better vibes, some "make fit mare Fancy me" vibes and can my gorgeous girl have some more just to make sure she comes home soon?

PS Poof bags has read somewhere about the power of mud packs in improving ones face - Mum didn't seem too amused though tonight when she saw what he'd done. Hee hee!!

27.11.2009

Dear Diary
This week has been a strange but good one. Firstly my beloved is home!

This has made me very happy, even happier when I saw she'd put on stockings for the occasion – oh boy! Thought I – but alas this appears to be a bandage and not an attempt to seduce me in a Mrs Jones type moment. Poo.

I am pleased she's back though Mum does keep saying this business about her not being out of the woods yet. What woods? She's in the stable? Lord I think my mother has taken a few too many blows to the head in her life.

Meanwhile I am still ill. The vet stole more of my blood this week so I am getting increasingly concerned it may be being sold on the black market. I would like it back at some point but apparently they're not going to give it me? Why? Its MINE. Life is so unfair.

Even more unfair is because I'm ill I'm not allowed to do any fast work or get tired. Yippee thought I – holidays and paaarrrtty. Alas no. My mothers idea of not working hard is to do lateral work. Lots of it. In WALK. I've not been this bored since the trip over from Ireland when I had to listen to the life story of the horse next to me all the way from Ireland to Derbyshire. Now THAT was boring. Why do I need to be able to leg yield, turn on my bum etc etc? I have managed all these years without doing so why now? I blame some cult place she went to the other week – it was somewhere in Warwickshire(?) and she came back all enthused.

Meanwhile at the yard it's all change. There are diggers and bumpers and big trucks and cement machines all over the place. It's very interesting. Well I think so. Poofy mean time is having apoplexy. Honestly I'm renaming him Poofy the magic dragon – the amount of snorting he's doing is ridiculous. I however keep testing the mens handy work. They're Irish and whilst I am Irish myself I do distrust men from the emerald isle who lay tarmac and things. So every day I go and put my foot on the curb stones they have laid and push on them. I like to think of it as quality control. They don't appear to share my sentiments. Ungrateful people.

So if next week I don't write these men may have given me some concrete wellies and used me as ballast.......

04.12.2009

Dear Diary

I think I preferred it when Mum thought I was very ill. This week the vets have told her that my blood work looks a lot better – whatever that's supposed to mean? How can my blood look better? Its still red isn't it? Very odd. This however has meant Mum has decided I'm not going to break if I do a bit more work. Ha! What does she know? I am a very delicate little flower underneath this manly exterior.....besides which I quite liked lounging around not doing a lot.

The vets have said she has to put this disgusting gloopy brown stuff in my tea and to start working me as normal. Apparently the stash of blood they have stolen will last until after Christmas because that's when they're coming back for some more. I hope they are rationing it well - I'm not in the mood to give them anymore just yet.

So WORK has started again. Boo hiss. Mum has been on a service to someone called jury the last few weeks so she has been at home. So I have been working again. Admittedly not that hard but still more than I would like AND making me do poncy dressage things.

Then Dad took me out for a hack round the block with old-but-still-quite-attractive mare. I can tell you she's quite the MILF. If its wasn't for my unrequited lust for fit mare I might be tempted to let her show me a trick or two I can tell you. We went out and it was nice and sunny, then halfway round it started raining – lots. Phew that girl could win some wet and wild contests – hubba hubba! I was so distracted I nearly fell over my own feet. Dad and Aunty Sarah however didn't seem to wish to hang about so we trotted down the drive which we never normally do. Then Aunty Sarah yelled "I'm not getting off out here it's too bad!" so THEN Dad rode me straight into the stables!! Without getting off!! He rode me into the stable and then jumped off like a cowboy. Daddy is SO naughty but its always great fun!! Even Mum was laughing despite nearly being flattened as I hurtled though the door.

Mum was not laughing the other night after I accidentally behaved like Poof bags and flattened her. Ooops. She was taking me out for a ride and the nasty concreting machine things and the diggers were there. The men jumped up and turned the engine off as we were coming past and the thing lurched for me. I thought it was going to eat me so decided to leg it – quite forgetting Mum was with me. Her language is SO impressive when she's mad. She knows so many words! Even more so as she was dancing on one foot at the time (apparently I'd stood on her toes). I did try to cuddle her to apologise later but she's still huffy with me.

58

SO because she's mad with me I don't trust her to convey the message I wanted to send to you lovely ladies. A few of you have asked for my address to send me cards for Christmas – if you email Mum she will act as my secretary and tell you where you can post them to. She may as well make herself useful............ [I'm now running before she reads that...............!!!]

Oh PS I forgot to tell you about my girl.

She's at home on box rest which means I get to stare at her (in a non-creepy way) all day. She's allowed to walk up and down for 10 minutes a day but Mum never lets me be there when that is happening. Apparently me taking the opportunity to bite her yummy bum when she's walks past isn't helpful.

Her stitches came out on Thursday and she is still wearing sexy stockings. I do however get to share my hay with her every morning for 10 minutes – she gets moved into the stable next to me whilst her Mum mucks her out. She still has not given in to my come hither glances but our lips did meet over the haynet yesterday. She bit me in fairness but I think she playing hard to get? What do you think?

14.12.2009

Dear Diary

I am so sorry for not writing on Friday but Mum had once again taken the laptop away with her and as such I was incommunicado for the day. I have asked Santa paws for a laptop for Christmas but Mum has said I'll be lucky if I get a carrot. This I feel is grossly unfair but heh.

So what has been happening this week?

Well as I think Mum has told you all my beloved girl was rushed back into horsepital and what a time of it Mum and her Mum had getting there! It sounded quite funny to be honest but then I wasn't stuck in a lorry on the side of the A1. I would have quite enjoyed it I think - I like nosing through peoples car windows when we stop in the lorry.

From what Mum has told me my girl has had another operation and is doing well. I'm hoping she will be home in time for Christmas because I have saved up and bought her a Swede. Well it's more like half a Swede now.......... I was hungry last night. In other news Poofy is away at naughty school. Dad finally decided that Poofy is indeed a big Poof and has sent him away to combat academy to toughen up (well I made that bit up but in my mind that's where he is). As I sat eating my hay in the warm the other night I had great fun imagining Poof bags running around an assault course and having to do press-ups. Then Dad ruined it and told me his stable is bigger than mine and he's getting two meals a day - excuse me?!! How does that work? I'm an angel (well sort of) and I'm only on one meal a day. The downside of Poofy being away is Dad has decided to help get me fit again after my time off due to being poorly.

I'm not sure I like this idea. He keeps making me go out on hacks on our OWN. The man is mad - how am I supposed to defend him against the lesser spotted wheelie bin without a wingman? As for taking on the rampaging tractors of terror alone - is he for real?! Mum also has said I'm going out next week for a little jump - I have heard ghastly rumours that they've bought me some antlers and Dad a Father Christmas suit. I am going to DIE if they have. Apparently the jumps are tiny but the kids will love seeing me. What me dressed up like an idiot with Dad equally looking like a spanner?! I also heard Dad tell someone he's bought Mum an elf costume. I'm not sure if Mum knows but I do know what's left of my standing in the area has now left the building.............
Anyone want to adopt me please so I can divorce my parents?

18.12.2009

Dear Diary
I hate my parents. Truly I do. I swear their sole purpose in life is to ruin mine. Take yesterday for example. It was snowing, freezing cold and generally very Christmassy. Mum brings me in a bit earlier than normal and I look forward to a night gazing lovingly at fit mare whilst impressing her with my wit and humour. Alas no, Dad brings in my tack and they spend ages fiddling with it. I spied something on my bridle as Mum put it on but it was too quick so I couldn't see.

Then fit mare starts sniggering……….. I still fail to see what is funny as Dad leads me out into the snow to the ménage. It's only when I catch a glimpse of myself in the window that I see…….. ANTLERS! Do I look like a chuffing reindeer? Eh? What in gods name are they thinking? I look a total idiot. Fit mare sang Rudolf the red nosed Hovis at me all night. There are times when I could go right off that girl.

Anyway what of the rest of the week? Well as can be seen from my heart break last night fit mare is back. She's had her operation and is back on box rest again. I'm keeping everything crossed that she will be well this time. The vets have said only time will tell. So go find this Time guy and ask him - we all want to know if she's going to be ok.

Poof bags is still at boot camp but I swear I heard Dad tell someone that's he's been hunting. I may be going a bit blonde like Mum but I swear that's what they call the big hacks with dogs that I've been on? If that's right how is THAT fair? I love those hacks with the forgetful dogs who keep losing the man in the red jumper. Why can't I go? Instead I'm stuck here being forced to canter on the correct leg despite my every effort to go on the leg I want to go on. They're my legs surely I should be able to choose? So how come he gets to do fun things at boot camp and I don't? I thought he was being beasted by a legion of evil people not allowed to go for nice trips out in the countryside. Life sucks.

As Mum wants to take me jumping tomorrow, later today Evil Army Man and Cool New Shoes man are coming. Together apparently. I am starting to worry about those two. Apparently Cool New Shoes Man heard about Mum parting company from me during our last army style beasting session and said it would be funny to watch. Ha. No one laughs at Mum but me Mr cool shoes man. So be careful I don't tread in something nasty just before you lift my feet up. Ha! I'm seriously tempted to pretend I can't remember how to jump so Mum won't make me wear those antlers in public tomorrow. What do you think.......?

31.12.2009

Dear Diary
My girl is gone.

My beautiful fit mare was put to sleep on Christmas Eve, after a hard fought battle to save her following a kick in the field. She was only 3 years older than me, life is so very very unfair.

My Mum and Dad were there with her and her Mum managed to get home from her overseas posting to say good bye.

I am lost without her. This is for you, my beautiful girl:

"Sleep tight my girl, in peace now rest
In loving you, I've loved the best
Your talent outshone others, outshone mine
You'll be in my heart for the rest of time.

If I close my eyes I see you still
And in my heart I always will
Your little socks and blaze so white
Coat shining like silk, dark as night
The most gorgeous legs I've ever seen
Going on for forever, long and lean.

Now I am heartbroken and left alone
Knowing the fields together we'll no longer roam
It seems to me you were only on loan
And God decided he wanted his angel home

I think your light too brightly shone
Now your time on earth with us is done.
But I know when I look up tonight
You'll be the star that shines so bright

Forever in my heart and in my mind
Ageless you are now, till the end of time
Be at peace now girl, running free
And when my time comes, return for me."

In loving memory of Minnie "Moo" Marshall. A stunning, amazingly talented girl
who's light was extinguished 24th December 2009.

Sleep tight Mooey.

2010

Dear Diary

I am aware that due to my misery over losing the love of my life at Christmas I have failed to tell you Poof bags has gone too.

Mum and Dad sent him to naughty school where it appears you get to do lots of fun things – like go on long hacks with those dogs and men in red coats. I was so disappointed – I thought he'd be doing squat jumps in the snow.

Apparently Poof bags showed a natural aptitude for chasing after dogs and someone made Dad an offer he couldn't refuse…. So Poof bags has gone to a new home where they will not make him try to be a show jumper (which to be fair he was PANTS at) and will let him go out with the dogs lots. I'm not sure that is very fair. I don't want to be a poncy dressage pony but that doesn't seem to stop Mum making me go round in lots of circles.

I miss him in so far as he was fun to wind up but Mum and Dad have promised me a new brother or sister – I'm hoping for a sister, as when my heart one day heals from the loss of my fit mare, maybe a sister could introduce me to some nice girls?

Anyway in an effort to be positive about the New Year and help me get over the death of my girl, I have made some New Years resolutions. I thought I would share them with you:

1. Learn how to ice skate – as this appears to be the only way any of us will ever get out of our stables and see grass again……..

2. Be nicer to my Mum – in case someone makes her an offer she can't refuse and I end up being a dressage princess for the rest of my life…

3. Learn how to cunningly swap legs whilst cantering so that Mum thinks we're on the right one and I'm on the leg I'm happiest on = both of us happy!

4. Perfect my commando roll to ensure both sides of my neck, body and face get equally covered in mud. Mum loves this and I want to make her happy (see number 2)

5. Try to keep Mum on my back when jumping over jumps. Apparently the name of the game isn't just to get over the jumps but to get Mum over them too. I wish

someone had pointed this out before then Mum wouldn't feel the need to question who my Dad was on a regular basis....

6. Help Mum with stable duties more – she enjoys it so much when I brush up with her, empty the wheel barrow or help her smash the ice in the field trough. Therefore I must do more of this to make her happy (see number 2)

7. Learn to throw a Poof bags inspired tantrum when asked to do anything resembling dressage – it worked for him and jumping so no reason it can't work for me and stressage...

8. Try to listen more to Mum: Remember that "whoa you big fat horse of unknown parentage" means she wants me to slow down. Try not to cringe at her appalling singing. Try not to snigger when I have swiped snot down her back without her noticing.

9. Fill my Diary in every week without fail – unless Mum has stolen the laptop.

10. Make 2010 the year of The Destroyer. Apparently monkeys, dragons and such like have their own year so I claim this one as mine!

08.01.2010

Dear Diary
I think the world has gone very strange in this New Year.

First of all there is a lot of the evil white stuff on the ground that we all know EATS horses. In fact there is that much of it that none of us have been out for weeks. It was kind of fun at first – like a big sleep over party but its getting really boring now. Plus I'm starting to get to know my fellow stable mates a little bit more than I think is healthy. Seriously some of them can fart for England. I know a touch of flatulence can't be helped but when they are holding competitions as to who can do the loudest one then it's offensive. That's before I mention some of the conversation topics. My young innocent ears are positively mortified as to what the older boys and girls have been talking about – I had NO idea that "jump" had a different connotation to the one where there's fences involved.

Mum and Dad come down twice a day to see me, make me move into wise old Timmys old stable so they can clean out mine and then the last few days they've been making me walk out into the white stuff! Do they not love me? Yesterday the white stuff was moving towards me all the time and I was not happy at all. Dad told me it was the wind and to stop being such a Poof. Its alright for him – he'd not suddenly grown 4 inches taller and wasn't trying to control 4 feet that suddenly had a mind of their own. Mum did get all the nasty white stuff out of my feet when I came back inside but still I think there was no need to put me in that kind of danger. I did briefly organise a "blow away the white stuff" party the other night but after two of us started hyperventilating and ginger-not-totally-wench-like mare fainted I figured we were fighting a battle we can't win.

Mum bought me a new treat ball to play with yesterday so I got my own back on all the farters by keeping them awake all night kicking it into the wall. Things went slightly wrong when a rather enthusiastic kick sent it into the air and into the water bucket Mum has put in for me. It's perhaps worthy of note that this does not aid retrieving the treats out of it – they swell up and then get stuck. I haven't been so frustrated since fit mare told me she was naked and Mum had put my rugs up so I couldn't see...........

Mum has told me her and Dad are still on the hunt for a new brother or sister for me since Poof bags departure but all the white stuff means that there's no point in going to see anyone as they won't be able to ride him or her. Now personally I think they're missing the point. I think to make up for my recent hardships I should be allowed to go with them and judge my new sibling on looks, character and whether I could kick their ass in a field fight. I'm fed up of always being the "little" brother. Whether they're any good for Dad to ride I personally think is irrelevant – heh if he wants talent he has me!

Anyway Diary until next week....I'm off to listen to the radio and encourage ginger mare with her New Year fitness plan..... pole dancing isn't quite what I thought it would be but a boy isn't complaining....................

15.01.2010

Dear Diary
Today is very exciting. I might be getting a new sister to try out. Well I think Dad is supposed to be trying her for a while to see if he thinks she's any good at SJ but personally I think Mum and Dad want to see if I like her.

Apparently that's only going to happen if she passes her vetting though. Seriously if she doesn't pass it she doesn't deserve to be called a sister of mine. When I had my vetting test the other guys at the yard told me what to do. So here are my tips for passing your vet test:

1. Don't bite the vet.

2. Don't kick the vet

3. Don't make the mistake of thinking the vet is moving in for a snog when they hold that funny light up to your eyes – take it from me they're not.

4. Don't think it's amusing to look cross eyed at the vet when they're studying you at close range. Apparently that can mean they think you're BLIND

5. When asked to trot in a line don't think its funny to change the beat of your foot sounds halfway down the yard. Whilst it's quite funny to see your Mums face the vet usually seems to think this means you are LAME

6. For once summon up the energy to lift your own feet up rather than expect the vet to do it. Humans apparently view this as a sign of something sinister – i.e. you are LAME. We all know it's more a sign of "I can't be arsed and you're daft enough to do it for me" but heh whatever works for them.

7. When the vet holds your leg up till its dead don't hop around the yard on 3 legs screaming like a girl for 10 mins afterwards. This apparently means you are LAME. Instead take it like a man and run off on all four legs whilst surreptitiously taking a note of the vets car registration number to arrange a small "accident" at a later date.

8. Try not to sound like you smoke 50 a day when asked to run round in circles – whilst it's apparently ok for Mum or Dad to be unfit and slightly overweight it's a complete crime if we are seen to be.

9. Deep sighing and snorting whilst running round in circles is not seen as you expressing your disgust at being made to run but may mean you have WIND issues. The fact most of the horses on my yard have wind issues and it's not from the front end seems to have escaped the attention of most vets I have met.

10. Finally one for us men only - if the vets asks you to cough whilst holding parts of your body that a man shouldn't hold, forget point 1 and 2 and beat the living daylights out of him. He's not really conducting a vet test and is possibly just a pervert.........
So we shall have to see if this girl can pass her test – I shall let you know soon. I don't know what she's called but I do know she is ginger. There goes my standing in the neighbourhood......again.

In the meantime the white stuff has continued to mean we can't go out. Mum takes me for walks in hand but its v v BORING. I thought it would be most fun to put my nose in the white stuff the other day and then flick my head up sharply thus covering Mum in snow. Note to self – don't do that again, that lead rope stings more when it's cold… Anyway until next week I leave you with my current conundrum. What do I do if this girl passes her vet test and she's a fox?

22.01.2010

Dear Diary

I do not have a new sister. The vets test was apparently too hard for her and the vets told Dad she wasn't as lovely as me. Well that's my take on what happened anyway. Personally I think she didn't live up to my high standards but it's a shame because Mum said she was sweet. She should have read my Diary last week then she might have passed the test.

Mum and Dad are therefore still looking for me a new brother or sister. They went to see a brother for me today, who yet again is GINGER! So's the one they're seeing next week. What's with the ginger ninja theme here? Seriously will one of you have a word with them? Poof bags ruined most of my reputation - having a ginga for a brother or sister will trample what's left of my street cred into the muck heap.

Anyway this week Dad has taken me out ALONE again TWICE! The man has a death wish. I need a wing man if we're flying missions in the woods - how am I supposed to spot the pheasants in the sun plus look where we're going? Instead of a wing man I get Dad singing with some girl who comes with us but is invisible - how does that work? I can hear her singing but I can't see her? Maybe she's really small and in his pocket? Weird. I wonder if Mum knows about her?

Mum came back yesterday and made me do LOADS of boring boring transitions but she has told me we're going out on Sunday so I was really excited. Until tonight she mentioned we're going to Evil Army Mans house. That's why I'm late tonight - Mum and Dad were "touching up my clip" so Evil Army Man doesn't think I'm "scruffy". SCRUFFY? How can anyone think I'm scruffy? Sexily tousled yes but scruffy no.

I'm hoping there might be some hot chicks there on Sunday which would make standing in the shower room shivering my bum off for an hour tonight worth it. I have a feeling though that I'm more likely to be announced in the British Dressage team than be allowed to pull...... Unless you count muscles then I'll be allowed to pull lots. I have a feeling having not seen me for a while Evil Army Man is going to make me work.... so if I'm not seen or heard of again after Sunday will one of you write something nice for my eulogy?

29.01.2010

Dear Diary

I hate my parents. They are horrible and I feel sick in the head. I need rescuing immediately; I need love and quite possibly counselling after what they allowed someone to do to me yesterday. Yesterday I was VIOLATED by someone pretending to be a vet.

Alright so maybe I haven't been weeing as much as I should have, maybe I'm not drinking like I should but really was there any need for Dad to drive me to a hospital and allow them to do things to me? Firstly a MAN played with my wee willie winkie. A MAN! How wrong is THAT! At least I thought the girl who has cool coloured hair might do it but really this was wrong on every level. Then they drugged me and did things to me. I had cameras up every hole of my body, I have been assaulted in every way imaginable and quite a few that we couldn't even begin to imagine. Is this not illegal in this country? I was almost too ashamed to come home – I certainly haven't told the lads what went on. Can you imagine the conversation? "Hi F what did you do today?" .. "oh I hung out, stared at some girls and ate grass. What about you?".. "oh I allowed a man to fondle my manly parts for the best part of half a day"………

I would never be allowed to play "I'm a stallion" with the boys again.

I am traumatised beyond belief. Anyway the upshot of all the horrific experiences was I'm a healthy boy with an infection in my wee pipe. I'm sure there must have been other ways to find this out. Sick individuals. Apparently I am still slightly anaemic. I'm not bl**dy surprised. My red blood cells did a runner at the sight of the first camera.

All in all Diary I am not happy. And that's before I mention the lesson at Evil Army Mans where they are trying to turn me into some dressage diva and didn't allow me to jump over anything or the horrible homework he gave Mum involving lots of circles or the horrible tasting stuff Mum and Dad gave me for breakfast this morning.. I hate my life. Pease please please will someone adopt me?

05.02.2010

Dear Diary

This week has been mostly fun after a horrible time last week (you'll have to read last weeks Diary as I cannot even bring myself to discuss it again).

This week I have finally achieved the turbo charged status that I have wanted for so long. I now know how my beautiful fit mare used to kick my bottom in stubble field races – she drank nice tasting stuff before we went out! After my horrific experience last week I think Mum and Dad felt guilty because Dad gave me this really yummy stuff to drink in two big tubs in my stable. Apparently it is called cordial. All I know is it tasted of apples and berries and it was really nice but best of all was the effect it had on my legs!!

On Saturday Dad took me round the big fields at the back of the yard and Mum came up with the thing that barks to take pictures of me. Well we had a nice little walk and I noticed how much my legs wanted to run so when Dad asked me to go a bit faster who was I to argue? Yeeeehhhaaaaa! I have never been able to run so fast! Dad was so excited too – he was squeaking with pleasure.......or maybe that was the air leaving his lungs as he tried to breathe against the G force? – I'm not sure. Dad and I did have a little disagreement about how far we should run but he came round to my way of thinking and we did 3 laps of the field at full tilt, cowabunga, feather flying warp speed. It was ACE!!

I am a little concerned that Mum and Dad didn't share my view point as that night they took away the nice tasting stuff. It's so unfair. For the first time I could whoop the bottom of anyone who wanted to challenge me to a race. I was going to change my name from "The Destroyer" to "The Feathery Flyer" (Do you like that? I thought it had a certain ring).

Alas when Mum took me out the next day my legs didn't want to run fast anymore? How does that work? I can still go fast for a big boy but I am no longer a blur streaking past at 1,000mph.

I have gone out on my own quite a bit this week with Dad as Mum has been away. We even went as far as the river bank all by ourselves (I have given up on trying to tell Dad we need a wing man as quite clearly he is mad). Whilst, as ever, I was a good brave boy I'm not happy with these new style puddles that seem to be all the rage at the minute. The ones that look like white hard stuff so you stand on them then they crack and you get wet feet. Personally I don't think that's sporting or funny. They could at least make the water in them warm rather than freezing cold.

69

I got all excited last week as Mum and Dad went to see a new brother who is YOUNGER than me. That would make my day as I'm fed up of being the little brother. Dad is apparently concerned he's too young though and I swear he said he's green. GREEN? I may be a bit thick but surely anything that's green is more likely to be an alien? Either that or he's got a seriously bad cold…….. Mum and Dad are going to see a potential new brother at the weekend that's a bit older than me but not by much so we'll wait and see. I hope they find someone soon as I much prefer going out with someone else. It gives me someone to roll my eyes at when Mum is singing.

Anyway I'll let you know how they get on next week. In the meantime does anyone know where I can get 4 tennis rackets and some string – the white stuff is back………….

12.02.2010

Dear Diary
I have a new brother! Although how happy I am about it is still up for debate. He arrived the other night and my first thoughts were he seemed quite cool but then he snored all night so I was not best impressed by the morning. Plus I had to lend him a pair of PJs as Poof bags old ones were too big.

When Mum and Dad came down Mum gave me lots of love but Dad went straight to see new Fancy pants so I think something needs to be done to remind everyone of the hierarchy around here. I get fuss first then everyone else. Like duh! It's not difficult. Well new boy is not as weak as he looks as he managed to break the stable chain and escape – I was quite impressed – I can't do that and I'm much bigger! Dad was not amused so that tickled me.

Anyway new bro's name is Pride which I think makes us sound like some sort of dodgy sliced loaf. Mum says he's the same age as me so I have to decide if I want to be the older brother or the younger one. That's a tough decision. If I say I'm older I have to be mature and "lead by example" but I'm fed up of being treated like the baby of the family. I'm at a loss as to what to do……..I can hardly say we're twins – my neck is twice the size of his!
Anyway I am concerned that this lad is as big a Poof as Poof bags was. Mum took me down to the field yesterday morning when all of a sudden there was a shout from behind us and Fancy pants shot past trailing his lead rope at full speed. I'll give him credit he is quite fast – mind you Dad was running pretty quick trying to catch him. Mum and I waited patiently for the pair of them to stop larking about and eventually Fancy pants came running back to me and Mum. Like I was going to save him – he

needs to learn fast it's every man for himself around here. Anyway he's up in the naughty "you might have germs so stay away from us" field for the next week so we shall see how he gets on. I think I might need to have a word about showing us up in front of the mares - I have enough problems pulling without him adding to my woes.

Mum and I might be going out for a little jump tonight at a little competition so I shall have to bring home a rosette to show Mr Dumbblood that us big boys can jump too – I won't stand for another brother of mine questioning my breeding. Ok maybe Mum wasn't fussy but that doesn't make me a bog trotting thicko. Apparently this Fancy boy is an eventer – I assume that means he thinks he's something special at cross country – well he's in for a shock. Nobody does cross country like I do it so stand aside posh boy and I'll show you how it's done. Anyway we'll see. I hope he chills out and we can have some fun together – as long as he remembers my simple rules we'll be fine:

1. Hay is mine. It doesn't matter if it's in your haynet – it's still mine.

2. All mares are mine. If you think they are making eyes at you, you are mistaken.

3. Grass – is mine. Unless I say you can have a bit. If I change my mind and want the bit you are standing on then you have to move. Immediately and without argument.

4. Water- the drinking trough is mine. I may from time to time allow you to drink from it but only if I'm in a good mood and you groom that hard to reach bit behind my ears.

5. The cool seats on the lorry are mine. I have shotgun rights at all times.

6. I don't like over familiarity – when it comes to names Sir Hovis is fine…

What do you think?!!

19.02.10

Dear Diary
I am worried. I think my new brother likes me. And I don't mean likes me I mean "likes" me. In the very wrong kind of a way. He's been allowed up from the "you might have germs and kill us all" field into the field next to us and he's become like a stalker. He won't leave me alone – it's so uncool. I mean it's nice to have a new

friend but seriously if the dude doesn't stop yelling for me all the time the mares are going to think I bat for the other team.

All in all it's been a good week despite Fancy pants braying for me like a seaside donkey the minute I move. Dad and I went up the fields on Tuesday and had a good blast around whilst he had a little "man to man" chat with me about behaving for Mum the next night. Now quite frankly I saw no need for this conversation I ALWAYS look after Mum – any midair dismounts that have happened have always been her fault not mine. Hey I always get safely to the other side of jumps – all she has to do is hang on.

Anyway the next night Mum upset me by washing my feathers in COLD water but then she saved me when I got my head trapped between the lead rope and the wall (note to self – don't do that again it was very uncool – I nearly wet myself in a style reminiscent of Poof bags).

We then loaded onto the lorry and set off. We got to a venue I vaguely recognised as the place Mum had made me trot about in covered in baby power and I was filled with dread. Then I saw army man and thought phew! Unless he's come over all weird on me then at least we're doing some jumping. I do think there must not be enough air at these places though because as soon as Mum goes anywhere other than the yard she starts breathing funny. It's most odd as Dad and I seem to be ok.

Anyway we walked up and then Evil Army Man began the beasting. There was me and another horse and he was making us work v v v hard but it was FUN! Yippee – boing boing boing!! Over jumps we went. Mum and the other horses Mum were puffing and panting like THEY were doing all the work after an hour! What on earth is that about? Hey it's my legs doing the running, my legs doing the jumping – not Mums? Anyway not-so-evil-army-man said I was fab so I have decided that I like him again at the moment. We're apparently going to his house again soon so I'm hoping he puts the kettle on – I have recently discovered "tea" and it's very nice. Mum was "over the moon" with me which I didn't understand as there wasn't a moon in sight – we were inside? The woman is most odd sometimes – I do love her but she's bonkers.

The other ladies horse was in trouble as she fell off over a jump so I was pleased to see it's not just my Mum that does these silly things.

Anyway I had the day off yesterday as Mum was moaning about how much her legs hurt – again – HELLLOOO!! It's MY legs doing the work woman – just sit there and let me get on with it. Army man says Mum has to trust me and that I am a darling –

note to EAM can you call me a dude or something not a "darling" - people give us funny looks.

Anyway at some point soon Fancy pants is coming into our field so I shall be keeping a close eye on him. So what the dude can jump 1.2 m jumps out of trot but I have bigger feet than him and will plant one on his nose if he tries any hanky panky with me!

So until next week this is the feather powered flyer signing off!

26.02.10

Dear Diary
I am concerned even more about my new brother. Last week I confessed I think he LIKES me and this week I have discovered he doesn't know how to play "I'm a stallion"! Every boy knows how to play "I'm a stallion" so perhaps he is a girl?

Anyway this week he has finally been allowed to come and play with us and be let out of the "you have germs and might kill us all" field. On the morning in question Mum gave me a big lecture about being nice to him whilst Dad wrapped Fancy pants in so much gear he looked like a bionic horse. My other two field mates looked the same – did I get any protection? Hum? NO! I can't decide if that means Mum doesn't love me or that she thinks I'm well hard.

Anyway we wandered down to the field and that funny white stuff that you can't see through was all in the air so I must confess I didn't even notice at first that Fancy pants was with me. I of course have told the others it was because I was being aloof and cool – not that I need to go to spec savers. Anyway my other two mates Felix and Shortstuff came along shortly and we all had a sniff and a run about. This seemed also to confuse his lordship as he stood in the middle not getting the idea that we were having a race – I'm seriously hoping he's not going to be a kill joy. Then I tried to get him to play "I'm a stallion" and he didn't get that either. In the end I went back to Mum to complain and see if she had any food.
Yesterday I went out with Mum and we went for a trot about in the field – I'm starting to think Mum is on that confidence stuff again because we were going quite fast and she didn't squeal once. I did get rather muddy though so when I got back I had to bite Fancy pants on the nose when he dared to suggest I should be used to mud being a bog trotter from Ireland. Hey Mr – I'm less of a mongrel than you are – warmblood ha!! Heinz 57 more like!

Anyway today I have had to babysit brother dearest whilst Aunty Sarah and Dad went out for a hack. I love my Aunty Sarah as she is v cool and likes to go fast but she is a bringer of rain. She is the rainmaker. Every time she rides me I end up soaking wet and covered in mud. Which does not bode well for later as I'm sure Dad said we're going out – more cold showers ahoy me thinks – yuck yuck yuck.

Anyway new bro was ok although someone needs to tell him that fallen branches are not snakes – chill dude it's the dive bombing pheasants you should be worried about and those evil wheelie bins not blinking branches. Sheesh. He got to wear a Fancy raincoat as well whereas yours truly had to get wet. Mum said it's because I am a big brave boy and don't need one – Dad says it's because my bum is too big to find one to fit. A boy can dislike his father at times……..

Aunty Sarah and I also showed him how to do cross country banks as we boinged up and down the bank like a big hairy rabbit on speed. Yeah stand aside "eventer" boy and let me show you how it's done.

Anyway I think I'm going out tonight and we might be going to see Evil Army Man tomorrow – I cannot wait to see what he does to Fancy pants, it's hard to look all Fancy and poncy when blowing like a 50 a day smoker! Hee hee! I haven't told him yet – I think I might let the experience be a "nice" surprise – does that make me a bad boy?

05.03.10

Dear Diary
I think my heart may be slowly healing from the loss of my beloved fit mare. On Saturday I found myself surrounded by girls and whilst none of them were as lovely as her, I did quite like a couple of them!!

Anyway I will explain. On Sat Fancy pants and I went to Evil Army Mans house for a lesson. He called me rude names as I got on the lorry so I spent the journey there trying to kill him. Unfortunately those dastardly bars between us prevented me ripping his head off but I had a good go none the less. When we got there Mum said I was going first so she led me off the lorry into Evil Army Mans yard. Cue Fancy pants throwing a MASSIVE strop. It was SO embarrassing. He was calling for me, jumping up and down and generally being a complete girl – I wanted to die. After a brief discussion (which to my disappointment didn't include an option to send him away to naughty school) EAM's lovely girlfriend took one of her mares out and let Fancy pants go into her stable. At least it made him stop yelling like a girl……..

Anyway I went to warm up and not-so-evil-army-man said we'd do some jumping. "Yippee" thought I. "Oh no" said mother "I want to work on my position today". WHAT?!! So instead of fun jumping we did boring boring boring walking and trotting with me having to hold my own head up and mother faffing about with her legs. The woman is such a killjoy. All this whilst being rained on – life is so cruel. I haven't even mentioned the fact she gave me a cold shower on Friday night then didn't even take me jumping. It was v windy and someone told her the warm up was outside so she wussed out. Oh and the fact she's hacked off my bum hairs with a pair of scissors "slipped", giggled and told me it'd grow out soon. My ass has steps up it like the stairway to heaven. I'm seriously hoping I'm wrong about my new brother otherwise I could be in BIG trouble. I think I'm close to being an RSPCA case……….

On Saturday after I was finished – an HOUR and a HALF later – I was allowed to swap places with Fancy pants and go into one of EAM's stables. That was quite cool. For a start someone had left all their hay in a big bucket thing on the wall rather than in a haynet – I want one of those things, it's SO much easier to fill your face than having to pull your tea out of little holes! Then I looked up and noticed all the GIRLS!! I had one either side of me, one in front of me – phewee! Hubba hubba was I happy or what?! If it wasn't for the fact I would miss Mum and EAM cannot be trusted not to a) snog my face or b) work me until I look like a TB, I would quite like to stay there. Maybe I could go on holiday there for a few days?

Anyway Fancy pants went off to do some work and apparently he jumped very high with Dad – about 1m Mum said. I have to say I thought that was cool so we became friends in the lorry until we got close to home and he suggested my bum leaning on the screens between us was too big and was squashing him. Ha! War then resumed until we got home……

On Tuesday Dad and I went on a fab hack together down to the woods and back and totally eradicated any trace of the nice clean feathers that Mum had worked so hard to achieve. Ha! That'll teach her to wash my legs in cold water and that fairy stuff! I'm not a fairy I am the destroyer and I look better covered in mud – it's far more manly.

On the way home we saw Mr W who owns the big house down the road – Dad and him stood talking and Dad said he'd got the horse equivalent of a range rover and a Ferrari. My question dear Diary, is which one am I?

12.03.2010

Dear Diary
Oh my lord what a week I have had.

First of all Aunty Mary and Uncle John came to visit at the weekend. Now last time I let Aunty Mary ride me I threw her off so I was under strict instructions from Mum to behave myself otherwise face her wrath. Now knowing Mums wrath usually involves the business end of a lead rope I decided that since my bum is now rather bald (see last weeks Diary for details), I would behave.

Anyway Aunty Mary rode me around a bit then jumped me over a few jumps. Just for fun I ran out on her a couple of times until I saw the look on Mums face, decided Mr lead rope might be about to make an appearance, weighed up my options of running quickly and then jumped everything. We then went for a play over the XC fences and the bank to show Aunty Mary how XC should be done when you have feather power. Yeehaa! I then took her for a run around the field and went back to bed.

The next day Mum and Dad loaded me on the lorry sans Fancy pants and we set off. Now I was a little confused as Mum wasn't wearing the pale coloured jodhpurs which I like to wipe my nose down so I didn't know what was going on. We got to a strange yard with lots of other horses and Mum let me off the lorry. Then she scared me to death by telling me she'd sold me!! NOT funny. It turns out we'd borrowed a riding schools ménage so I could get used to being away from home – heh Mum its not me that needs to get used to it. Do you see me breathing like a dirty phone call every time we set foot off the yard? Huuumm? Nope that'd be you Mum. Anyway there were lots of little people at this place who all thought I was fab so I pranced about showing off then Dad got on and showed them how high I can jump. They were all most impressed and gave me carrots and things. I quite like it there I have to say.

Then on Wednesday I had an awful trauma. I'm not even sure I can talk about it. My young brain is scarred for life……. Dad and I were out for a hack around the block when up in front we saw two cars parked in a layby. I thought nothing of it as we were on the way home and I was dreaming of bed and dinner. As we got closer a human female got out of one car, bent over "winked" like a mare in season at me then pulled her pants back on! I didn't know where to look! Dad by this stage was giggling to himself and made me ride right up to the car window where there was a man with his trousers not where they were supposed to be! Oh my Gosh!! He looked very embarrassed; Dad seemed to find this very funny and phoned Mum whilst we rode past. I'm sure he told her we'd just been "dogging"? Aren't dogs those things that bark? Trust me I didn't see any of them in the car or that would have been even more wrong. Some people are just weird. I told Pride about it when we got back and he was horrified too. He'd be even more worried if he'd overhead Dad say he was going back for another look!

Tomorrow I'm off to a dressage test then on Sunday I'm off to Evil Army Mans house and THEN on Monday I'm off to Cool New Shoes Mans house to have some new shoes fitted. I am such a jet setter! Cool New Shoes Man says I can relax in the heated solarium whilst he does my feet, see finally someone is realising how a star like me should be treated. Bliss!

19.03.2010

Dear Diary

What an interesting week I have had. As I told you in last weeks Diary Mum had planned a busy few days for me which started with the dreaded cold bath on Friday night. After strict instructions to levitate all night thus not getting my newly white feathers dirty Mum returned in the morning. Unfortunately so did the men with the concrete lorries, the mixers, the rollers and the big trucks.........

After much swearing Mum took me across some very nasty uneven ground and loaded me onto the lorry with a dumper truck running at the side of the ramp. Now I have to point out not many boys would have calmly walked up into the lorry with such a scary beast rattling away inches from their legs so I was feeling rather pleased with myself.

We got to the place we were going and I noted Mum had put on those nice clean jodhpurs that I like wiping my nose down so I was very excited. So was Mum judging by the language she used when Dad informed her I was on three legs with a back shoe hanging off...........So we turned round and came back home again. Dad then swore constantly for 10 minutes whilst he removed both my back shoes and the large piece of concrete that was wedged under my left back shoe.

Anyway I was sort of relieved not to be poncing around in circles and was v excited about going to Evil Army Mans house the next day.

Next day came and Fancy pants and I got on the lorry, we were closer together than normal – something I didn't understand until we pulled up on another yard and a strange mare got on.... She was with Aunty Sarah and her name was Snazzy (or something like that). It turns out she is Aunty Sarah's new team ride and is an ex-eventer at a high level but best still she didn't Fancy my brother!! Yippee!! Finally I have a brother whom women don't swoon over. In fact she tried to eat his head most of the way to Evil Army Mans house. Hilarious.

When we got to Evil Army Mans house I got off the lorry and headed for his ménage looking forward to a morning of jumping and lots of yeehaa cantering. Alas no. He seems fixated with the idea of me poncing about carrying my own head at the minute. What's wrong with the man? What happened to him? I think he might have had a bang on the head.

Why is it that Fancy pants got to jump? Huumm? Though he and Dad did part company so maybe they might have to do boring flat work too next time? Meanwhile Snazzy and I got cosy on the lorry whilst Fancy pants was riding and she's pretty cool for an older lady. Mum told me to stop drooling as she was old enough to be my grandma but heh I'm not fussy I can snog a GILF, I don't mind.

Snazzy went off for her lesson – flat work too I noticed and Fancy pants and I had a brief chat about not ruining my chances of scoring on the way home. Alas he fell out with her and I'm not sure if I'll see her again. Ah well we had a brief moment over the haynet so I guess that'll have to do.

On Monday we went to Cool New Shoes Mans house to be shod. OMG. Mum needs to start shoeing horses – his house is AMAZING!! I got to be shod in this cool little room with a heat thing soothing my muscles – it was v relaxing. Less relaxing was his stallion breathing down my neck in a very unmanly fashion. Cool New Shoes Man said the stallion might prefer men so I am now very very very scared. He kept calling to me and wiggling his top lip in a camp manner. Seriously dude there were women about – pull yourself together. I am starting to think I must give off more camp signals than an Indian Teepee convention. Why do men always like me? Fancy pants was in trouble for being a fidget bottom and trashing the yard. I was of course on best behaviour and everyone loved me – it's only natural after all.

Anyway Diary I think Mum said I could have some fun this weekend and go and play on my XC bank so I'm off to start practising by jumping over Fancy pants shadow on the grass. Laters........

My first day out chasing the man in the red jumper

Dad and I tackling the baby bank

Me saving Dad from the coffin at the cross country course *(photo with kind permission of Steve Wellburn)*

The antlers my evil parents made me wear

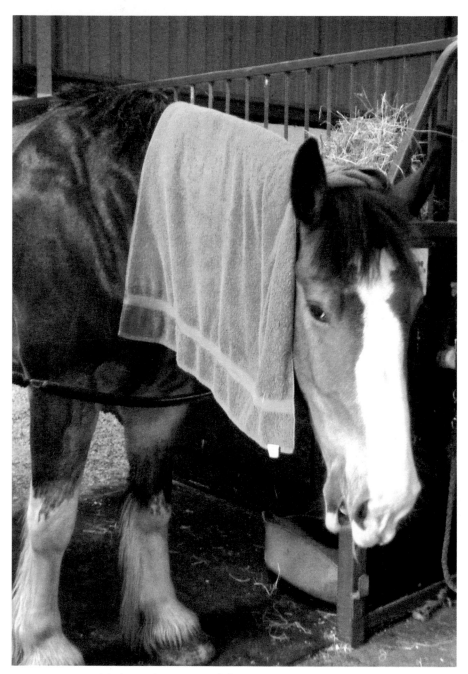

My boxer impression following yet ANOTHER bath

Me showing my opinion of dressage

Stand back Moorlands Dorrito, this is how you do it!

Photo: Simon Orr

Mum and I at one of our Show jumping "shows"

My beautiful fit mare

Mum and I having a cuddle in the white stuff.

26.03.2010

Dear Diary

This week I am mainly feeling smug. This is because I have been a good boy all week and Fancy pants is in the dog house after chucking Dad off again on Wednesday. Mind you I teetered on the brink of being sent to the dog house by Mum at the weekend but managed just to get back into her good books in time. Phew!

On Sunday Mum took me up to the big field for a play – now its was my fault but I do tend to think that big field is for one thing only – running like a bat out of hell round and round and round. Unfortunately Mum didn't quite see my point of view and after unsuccessfully trying to keep me in trot rather than full on yeehaa hold-onto-your-hairpiece-canter she gave up and made me walk instead. How dull….

Luckily I did recognise the signs that she was less than amused and so walked out like a good boy all the way home – phewee. A verbal tirade involving questioning my parentage duly avoided!

On Tuesday Dad and I went for a nice hack out down to the big woods and then around the block. I did avert my eyes in case we saw anymore naked naughty nookie people but thankfully they'd obviously found somewhere else to go and make babies.

Then on Wednesday Fancy pants made his HUGE mistake. I have tried to tell him the last brother that didn't behave was sent away to naughty school so he'd best start behaving. After Dad had removed himself from the large crater he'd made in the school Fancy pants was lunged until he was so tired he hurt nearly as much as Dad did and then sent to bed. Tut tut. At this point I adjusted my halo, smirked, forgot myself and bit Dad on the bum. He was last heard muttering something about hating horses…….

Mum came home yesterday and let me have a jump for the first time in ages last night which was great fun. She and Dad were working on lengthening and shortening my strides – what is with that? I don't care how many strides they say it is – I am the Destroyer and will do it in as many strides as it needs – which to be fair usually is at least one less than everyone seems to think it is. I have big legs what can I say?! Mum jumped me for ages and then Dad got on to show her how few strides we could make a four stride jump in. I tried for one but it was too big to bounce so I managed it in two. Mum did comment that there may have been news of an earthquake in the area on the television last night as I really thundered between the jumps to do it in so few strides. After that everyone said how clever I am and that I am a total star. Ker-ching! Take note Mum and give me some more dinner!

Anyway later on today my masseuse is coming (well Mum says she's a physio but since I am far too manly to ever have hurt myself she just gives me a nice massage instead). I am secretly hoping for a sick note but can't see it happening so alas I can see more poncing around holding my own head coming up this weekend. Sometimes being perfect has its downsides..........

02.04.2010

Dear Diary

Today is both an exciting day and a very sad day. Today Fancy pants and I move to a new home.

Mum asked me a while ago to not write about what was happening at my current home so I know this may come as a shock to you all. For a while now Mum and Dad have been picked on by a nasty person at my current home and it got so bad it was making my Mum cry a lot. So she and Dad have been looking for somewhere else for us to live where there is not this nasty person. The reason I've not been posting about some of my old friends from my home for a while is that they have all left too. In fact the stables have been getting emptier and emptier so it seems now it's our turn to leave...........

So today we pack our bags and go. I'm excited because I'll make some new friends, get a new room and find lots of cool new places to go out hacking. But at the same time I'm very sad too. This was my first home with Mum and it has a lot of memories for me:

This was the first place Mum brought me when she bought me, the first place I fell in love and the first place I lost friends:

This is the place my first brother broke his leg and the last place he lived before he went off to retirement.

This is the place Bertie and I first played "I'm a stallion", stood shoulder to shoulder dribbling water down our chins, frolicked in the snow and the place I last saw him before he went over the bridge without me.

This is the place I first saw my beautiful fit mare who will forever be the love of my life. This was the place I fought over her with Poofbags, gazed adoringly at her across the stables, went for long walks together with her in the woods and the place she broke my heart in two when she died.

This was the place Mum has laughed so hard at me she has cried, the place where I found out about the dog house, the place where cold baths have been the fashion, the place we have hunted for eggs, the place where Mum forgot her age and played silly games involving scary flags………..the place where for a long time we have had fun and the place I turned from a baby into a man.

I will miss this home and I know Mum will too but maybe now she will stop being so sad. I think it's sad that you humans can be so nasty to each other – what's wrong with having a quick bite and a kick and then it's all over? I guess the good thing is I will forever have my memories and my friends will come with me in my heart.

So it's on to pastures new – quite literally – and new adventures for Fancy pants and I. I am trying to remember all my bits and pieces whilst licking the stable stains off my knees in case any of my new dorm mates are female and hot. So Diary should I take gifts with me or wait until I have assessed them for looks and willingness to drop down the social register and frolic with me? Oh and is it a social faux par to ask them their age and how many kids they've had within 5 minutes of meeting them?!! Help!

09.04.2010

Dear Diary
Well what an exciting week I have had. As I told you all last week Fancy pants and I have moved house.

The day started with Mum and Dad chucking us out in the field whilst they packed up all our things, then we leapt on board our lorry and set off. Aunty Sarah came with us to help Mum and Dad so I could see her and Mum in a car following us as we drove along.

It didn't take long to get there and we jumped off to see a field FULL of lovely grass, I've never seen grass like it. Wowee! Dad took Fancy pants and Aunty Sarah led me down to the field which we were told was all for us! I could see some of my new room mates but to be honest I was more interested in the GRASS!! Fancy pants and I are now in a field by ourselves but we can see all the other horses over the fences. Now I have learnt a lesson about fences. These fences at our new home looked pretty puny… so I leant on one………….OUCH!! These fences BITE! How mean is that? So I told Fancy pants to reach under one wire to get some grass and he got stung too!! Hee hee!! I find me SO funny…

Anyway our new stables are cool, although I can't see through the sides of them like I could at my old house. My next door neighbours are both blokes and seem quite cool although I am concerned that one of them is as big as me (although older) so might eat all the grass. Opposite is a rather cute looking girl and Fancy pants has another girl next door to him. She's in the field next to us and has a very nice sleek bottom. She seems to like showing her bottom to me but I'm not quite sure what that means?

Mum seems to be concerned that we might not have anything to play with because she and the boss lady put a cone in our field in a big hole that the last horse in the field had dug. I think the cone is ace fun and so far have managed to put it in lots of hiding places. Mum loves this game and spends ages looking for it. She uses those words that she saves for special occasions and on Monday accidentally dropped the cone in an action that might have looked to the uneducated like she was trying to throw it at me.....

Then on Monday Fancy pants and I discovered that the fence wasn't biting the way it had been doing so we got major kudos from the other horses by appearing really hard and reaching under the wire to grab our box which is outside near the gate. We then played with our head collars and the brush and bucket that Mum and Dad had put there to clean out the trough. Unfortunately as Fancy pants and I were playing "clean up" with the brush and the tub, Mum and Dad came down the drive in their truck. Ooops! They then realised that the fence was playing nicely and so told the boss lady. She then obviously told the fence to man up because it's started biting really hard again. Poo.

Mum rode me on Sunday in the new ménage which is nice to walk on but is a little bit smaller than the one I've been used to. I don't mind though because it's next to the hay barn so every time I come down that side I open my mouth in the vain hope some might jump out and land between my teeth. Alas this has not yet happened. I got the day off on Monday, then Mum rode me again on Tuesday and Dad on Wednesday. I am a little aggrieved about this – I know I'm getting more grass but this doesn't mean they have a right to work me into the ground! Lots of my new room mates don't have to work as hard as me. Life stinks.

Even more stinky is that Fancy pants has a claim to fame. He was at the vets in the week for the vets to check out his back and someone called Polly Jackson rode him. He has not shut up about it since. She apparently said he was lovely, well schooled and had a "nice soft mouth". Ha! She's obviously not been bitten on the bum by him. Soft! Not likely. So do any of you know anyone famous who might want to come and ride me?

16.04.2010

Dear Diary

I am writing this from within a kennel. I believe that's where dogs live and I am in the dog house. Big time. I shall explain why in a minute.

Last Friday all was well with the world, the sun was shining, I was naked, eating grass, hanging out with Fancy pants and trying to ogle the girl in the next field without being too obvious. When a car came down the drive. HIS car. I had prayed with all my heart that when we moved Evil Army Man wouldn't know where we had gone so thus couldn't come and beast us silly. Drat it though the man found us and made me spend an hour prancing about like some queen dressage pansy with my head on my chest, CARRYING my own head. Someone report the man to the RSPCA. I have a BIG head. It's heavy. I shouldn't be made to carry it – that's what Mums are for. She in fairness was puffing and blowing like she was doing something difficult so he made her get off. Now to those of you who have never met EAM all I can tell you is that when he strides towards you and puts his foot in a stirrup its time to start praying. Needless to say I am no feathery fool so instantly I decided that carrying my own head wasn't so bad after all and proceeded to do my best impression of the dressage fairies I have seen at competitions. Mum started using all sorts of rude words but whether they were aimed at EAM or me I'm not sure........ maybe both of us?

Then he made her take me down the road on our OWN. The man is a sadist. I love my Mum dearly but seriously she is no use to me fighting one of those big tractor things. Luckily we didn't see any so all was ok but it was a close run thing.
Then all weekend Mum practised what EAM had shown her. Not content with ruining my Friday he ruined my weekend too. Seriously Mum is turning into a right teachers pet. To compensate Dad did take me for a quick hack and we had a great yeehaa canter up a track. That was fun. The rest of the weekend sucked.

Wednesday night Dad took me in the school and made me do lots of boring transitions including trot to canter. So I got my own back and refused to go on the correct leg. This went on for a while until I realised I was in danger of missing tea if I didn't play ball so then showed him I can do it when I feel like it.

That's another thing. All the other people at our place are being made to stay out at night. Do you think their Mums don't love them? I'd FREEZE if I had to stay out at night and there's no way I am sleeping with Fancy pants to stay warm. Sod Darwin's theory of intelligent beasts staying alive – I'd rather be extinct than wake up cuddling Pride, with him slobbering in my ear. Mum says when the weather is a bit warmer we can stay out if we want. Ha! Not bleeding likely mother. I like my bed and my PJs and my hay and having some "me" time away from his lordship.

Anyway yesterday morning I was roused out of my bed by Mum and Aunty Sarah. Aunty Sarah took Pride and Dad took me to keep them company on a little hack. This is apparently because I am "sensible". Yeah. About that…….. Now I swear I was not scared as that would be unmanly, I was concerned the tractor driver was lost so I was trying to show him the way. So to do that I HAD to take both my front feet off the floor…. and spin round to point……..

Dad is not amused, Mum is not amused, Aunty Sarah seemed to think it was very funny. Dad did suggest he was amazed that I could get my front feet off the ground in the first place, even if it was only a little tiny bit. So if you never hear from me again I have not escaped from the dog house. Can someone please smuggle me a carrot as I think the likelihood of me getting any in my tea tonight are something akin to zero………

23.04.2010

Dear Diary
I think my parents hate me. After last week when I stood up and directed the tractor, I think they have decided that the only course of action left open to them is to kill me. This week has been horrific, I have been to hell and back, Dad and Aunty Sarah have pushed Fancy pants and I to the limits of our endurance. I am mentally exhausted and traumatised beyond words. Ladies I need some loving to get over it all – any volunteers?

At the weekend Mum rode me in the school and we did some boring trotting poles, then some jumping which was fun. Then the next day Aunty Sarah rode Fancy pants and Dad took me and we went out for a lovely stroll in the countryside learning our new surroundings. It was v nice so when Aunty Sarah came again on Wednesday morning I was excited to be going out for another mooch. Alas father and Aunty Sarah had other ideas and put us through the most traumatic experience of my life!

First of all we rode down to this part of the road that had big gates on it. I was intrigued as to what they were trying to stop from escaping – well I soon found out! Great big steel snakes with lots of bodies parts that slide along metal poles hidden in the ground!! OMG! It was HUGE! And loud. I would have wet my knickers if Fancy pants wasn't too busy wetting his instead. Then when the snake had gone away we had to cross over its lair. I wasn't at all keen on this idea but faced with the prospect of Mr. Whip being landed on my bum I led the way across. Fancy pants let me get across to see if the snake ate me then legged it across too. Chicken.

Then we got to this track which seemed fine so once again I led the way with wimpy Pride practically clinging onto my tail hairs. I stepped out and........ nearly died. The ground literally moved under my feet. I couldn't contain myself and leapt forward as if Fancy pants had bitten my bum. It was only when I had shot forward several paces I realised the ground was in fact made up of pebbles and that's why it had moved. I am so glad there were no girls there to see Fancy pants and I jigging about like lizards on a hot tin roof. It was SO uncool.

By this time I was starting to think all of this was perhaps a cunning plan to see which one of Fancy pants and I was the toughest, with the wimpiest being packed off to be never seen again. So when we got back to another crossing across the metal snakes lair I calmly led the way across. Copy cat Pride followed my lead so we strode like MEN across the ground. Only for us both to leap out of our skins like girlie mice accidentally walking into a Whiskas convention when a big lorry came round the corner....... My street cred by this time was out of the window. We finally got home in one piece (just) and Dad and Aunty Sarah said we'd both been really good. I so wanted my Mum. She never does these mean things to me. Well so I thought till she schooled me for an HOUR last night prancing about doing boring boring transitions and making me canter slowly. SLOW canters? Isn't that like the most stupid thing ever?

This morning Aunty Sarah and Dad rode us out again and apart from a brief moment when I thought a van might be coming to eat me all was cool with the world. I heard Mum saying that she's going to take me out with the other big boy (my next door neighbour Billy) on the yard which pleased me immensely – snakes prefer bigger things to eat so it'll get him before it gets me.

Other than that life has been pretty cool. The grass here is v good, I have learnt to keep away from the fences that bite and I think I'm making progress with the mare in the stable across from me. If I can just get the older dude in the stable next to hers out of the way for a while then I might be able to show her that once you've had some Destroyer lurve you never want another. Any suggestions of how to do this?

30.04.2010

Dear Diary

I am sorry for writing my Diary late today but I have been at bereavement counselling. Even after today I am desolate, inconsolable and beyond comfort. This week I have murdered my new little friend. I didn't mean to, it was a dreadful accident, but I should be punished for my heinous crimes. How was I supposed to know little mice don't know how to do the river dance? When he started jumping about around my water bucket my mind was instantly transported back to the emerald isle of my birth and I joined in. With disastrous consequences………. I console myself with the fact that he died quickly. My 2/3 of a tonne weight poised delicately on one leg landing firmly on his head mid enthusiastic dosy do, sent him to mouse heaven quite quickly. I am a bad horse

In an unrelated incident Pride and I nearly sent Dad to human heaven. Luckily it appears the fences that bite do make humans squark rather loud but they don't kill them. Which is good……….. The fact the fence bit him on the bum actually was quite funny but as Pride and I had shoved him into aforementioned fence we did have to run away before we laughed too hard. I know how good a shot Dad is with lead ropes!

Dad isn't too chuffed with me this week as he took me out on my own on Weds without a wingman and we saw lots of those huge scary tractors. Now admittedly there was probably no need for the totally hissy fit in the middle of the road but since Fancy pants gets away with I thought I'd have a go too. I have since learnt that hissy fits hurt my bum. I'm not sure how the two things are related but I can assure you they are. My bum is still stinging…..

Mum was home yesterday and Cool New Shoes Man came to give me some cool new shoes. I was feeling in quite a loving mood so kept leaning fondly against him and licking his back. Judging from the things he said and his heavy breathing I think he quite enjoyed these brief cuddles. I quite liked them too as it meant he held me up for a few minutes so I could take a load off. He didn't half go a funny colour though. Maybe he was embarrassed by this public display of affection?

Anyway I am writing this whilst shivering as Mum was mean and put me out without a coat on this morning. Can one of you suggest she looks at the television thing that I hear other peoples Mums talking about which tells you the weather? A boy could get a chill. Just because I look well hard doesn't mean to say I am. I am a delicate little flower really………just a large ginger delicate flower……with big feet…..that kill little mice.

07.05.2010

Dear Diary

I am fed up. I am fed up of being seen as the "bog trotter" whilst my last brother and my new brother are seen as the handsome, poncy, arty farty, flowing paced, talented four legged teachers pets.

All week all I have heard is how wonderful Fancy pants is, how nice his paces are, blah blah blah! I have nice paces – a slow one, a medium one and a fast one. How many more does a boy need? I also don't scream like a girl if Mum leaves me in a field on my own, don't poo my pants if a worm sticks its head out of the ground and don't shiver pathetically if it rains. Do I get any appreciation? No.

I want a fan club. I want instructors to coo over me. I want the new boss lady at our yard to like me instead of Fancy pants. But I am buggered if I am prancing about like a fairy to achieve this.

Anyway we are off to Evil Army Mans house tomorrow so I'm hoping we get to do some jumping so I can show off my talents. Mind you Fancy pants swot head is pretty good at that too. Dammit I dislike him.

This week Dad has been working hard on brother dearest so I've had a pretty chilled week. We went out for a hack yesterday which was great fun – that's one thing I do far better than Fancy pants – I AM the ultimate all terrain vehicle. At the weekend Mum made me run round in circles with my head tied to my body. I don't think she's forgiven me for spitting water all down her back on Saturday. She should have moved quicker…..

This morning grandma came to visit from that hot place she lives in. I don't think she likes me. She came into the field with Mum to pick up our poo and squawked like a bird every time I went near her. I could have sworn she called me a clod hopping lump but I can't be sure. She is a small person but even I wouldn't tread on her unless she did something bad – like refuse to give me a polo mint.

So today I am mainly sulking whilst Fancy pants ponces about with his head getting bigger by the minute. If any of you feel you would appreciate me more than I am being appreciated here I am open to suggestions of a new home.

14.05.2010

Dear Diary

I have had a mixed week – in some ways I have had great fun, in others I have been traumatised and violated beyond words.

Get comfy and I will explain……….

On Saturday morning Mum, Dad and grandma arrived and loaded Fancy pants and I onto the lorry. I was a little dubious about this as it was raining quite a lot, but under the assumption my mother knows what she is doing, I ambled onto the lorry quite happily.

We arrived at Evil Army Mans house and brother dearest was tacked up and went off to the ménage. As it was still drizzling with rain I happily stood on the lorry eating my hay and generally mooching. I also sniggered as Fancy pants had to do a flat work lesson whereas Mum had promised me some jumping – yippee! However the sniggering came too early as when it was my turn to go out the heavens opened and the rain decided to attack me sideways not just from above. Evil Army Man did say I did the most impressive half pass he's ever seen from a big horse – a half what? All I knew is that I couldn't even see where we were going. Even the Evil one himself took pity on me and allowed Mum and I to go and stand under his barn till the worst of the rain passed.

We then did some jumping! He was mean to Mum, told her to grow a set and we did a little course in canter (she usually wusses and jumps in trot). From the way she was breathing I think Mum really enjoyed herself – well I know I did! Why her legs were shaking so much she had to hang onto me when she got off I have NO idea. It was hardly like we were doing puissance – although I do Fancy that too. Mum is funny sometimes.

After my exertions on Saturday Mum let me have Sunday off which was cool and then she went back to Scotland. That's when it happened……….. The final proof my brother is a big Poof and the most traumatic experience a young boy can imagine………..

It all started off so innocently – we were playing in the field, larking about when all of a sudden he, well he… he man mated with me! I have never been so shocked in all my life. For a second I thought I was imaging things but no! The dude was giving me some full on man love. Now I'm a willing to try anything kind of a guy (see pictures from last Christmas of me sporting antlers if you don't believe me) but seriously this was awful. Needless to say a swift kick removed him and he tried to pass off the whole thing as a bit of fun. FUN! For who? I have enough issues with the ladies without them seeing that little performance. Since then he hasn't tried it again but I have started grazing with my bum to the fence. Hey I'd rather get voltage up my bottom than a Pride surprise again. I think the dude has issues. I mean I'm all for a game of "I'm a stallion" but the whole point is we're BOTH stallions. Not him be the stallion and me be his conquest. I'm his BROTHER for the love of god.

Anyway yesterday I went out for a lovely hack with Dad and Aunty Sarah in the sunshine. I did keep a wary eye open for both tractors and Pride launching a rear guard action again but all was fine. We had a lovely canter but I'm not liking this new "canter up the only hill in the area" malarkey. Why can't be walk up and canter back down? So much easier I feel. The downside to our lovely hack was I appeared to have robbed the local area of all the sticky buds and hidden them in my feathers. Quite when that happened I have no idea but Mum seriously needs to learn to handle those bad boys a little bit better – my feathers now look like I have mange. So I can thus suggest that my chances of pulling at my new home are something akin to zilch – I have a brother who screams like a girl when I'm not there and doesn't seem to understand that that kind of brotherly love is wrong, Mum has pulled my mane so I look like a basin head and now I have manky feathers. Life at time sucks……………..

21.05.2010

Dear Diary

Well I am pleased to announce I have survived a week with no more incidents involving my brother. I am however now dying of heat stroke as God appears to have turned the oven up. We boys from the emerald isle are not built to cope with Sahara style heat waves. I am wilting away in a pile of my own sweat. I am trying to ensure I keep my nose out of the sun and thus not burnt before Mum makes me wear that mask thing again and any hope I might have of pulling Crazy Daisy vanishes like a carrot near Fancy pants mouth.

Last weekend Mum, obviously buoyed up by my superb jumping the week before, decided to jump me again. In canter……across an angle……….over a very high cross pole….. Now if she can't get me there straight how was I supposed to know we were aiming at the low part of the cross not the top of the poles near the wing? Mum squawked like a goosed chicken and did an inspection of my ears mid jump. As we landed I did notice Mum was now swinging around my neck like a very large ungainly human necklace so I duly stopped and allowed her to sort herself out. It's a good job I am the patient type. Seriously Mum it's not difficult – I jump the jump, you hang on and don't end up over my head. Sheeesh.

Anyway we have now gone back to jumping in trot in preparation for a show tomorrow. I'm fairly sure by "show" Mum means we're going to be competing against ponies that barely reach my knee caps again but heh if I get polos I can swallow the shame. Mind you I'm still smarting over the fact she made me practise last night in 100 degree heat. I could have DIED. It's surely cruelty to expect me to jump over things when its 110 degrees. She did give me a nice cold shower afterwards which sort of made up for it but I still think she has an evil streak. Note to self though – whilst having a bath don't keep trying to open the boss ladies wheelie bins with your mouth. For some reason it causes your bottom to sting. Clever things those wheelie bins.....

Today we are moving field which is great. I get nearer to the girls and we have loads more grass to eat. I like this new place we live – there's always loads of grass. I am not happy that Fancy pants is staying at home tomorrow eating all the new grass whereas I have to go and sweat my whatsits off cavorting around with small children and fences that Mum could jump over let alone me. Maybe I could suggest that? I'll jump on her back and she can run around the jumps? What do you think? Failing that do you think there's any chance of her mistaking Fancy pants for me and taking him instead? Suggestions please.

28.05.2010

Dear Diary
Well last week was interesting! As I told you Mum had told me she was taking me to a "show". Now I strongly suspected that this meant we were going to play with small ponies, small children and jumps that came up to my knees. I was right.

However what mother hadn't realised is that the play area was on grass. Now I LOVE grass. It tastes nice, it's nice to lie on, looks pretty and is generally lovely stuff. But Mum seems to hate jumping on the stuff. This could, in fairness, have something to do with the fact last time we jumped on grass we had a small disagreement over the line over a fence – I went one way, she went the other. Anyhow I digress.

We got there, Aunty Sarah and Dad unloaded me, Mum went off somewhere to be sick, wet her pants or some other such like and I set about eating grass. After much angst, heavy breathing, shaking and generally behaving like a girl Mum decided she wasn't going to wuss out and went to pay for our play session. Now I have to say by this time I wasn't too fussed. There were a couple of cute girls to look at, the grass was very nice, the sun was shining and I had seen someone walk past with an ice cream so was fairly sure I might convince Aunt Sarah to buy me one. Whether we jumped or not was immaterial – I was having a lovely day out. It was made nicer by the fact Fancy pants had been left at home in the dog house so I was being spoilt all by myself.

On the way there I had seen a sign for a happy hen farm which said – "1000 happy chickens and three ecstatic roosters". Does this mean there are places where you can go and there are 1000 girls to three boys? Wowee! I so want to go there. I did kick as we passed it on the way back to signal to Dad I quite liked the idea but no one seemed to pay any attention.

Anyway Mum came back from paying for our play time, tacked me up and took me to the warm up ring. Here she did her best impression of puff the magic dragon, breathing so deeply I though she was having a heart attack. She was all "easy boy, good boy" to me. Ha! I wasn't the one busy wetting my pants. She reckoned I was snorting and scared. No Mum that is my "I am a stallion, look at me ladies" snort. You crooning "steady boy" every two minutes makes me look a right plank.

Anyway Dad eventually prised Mum out of the warm up by pointing out that I would die of exhaustion before we jumped unless she got herself together. So to the accompaniment of mother heavy breathing and lots of the cries of "isn't he gorgeous" – why yes people I know – we set off. Now all was fine until I got a bit distracted over fence 3, saw Dad and Aunty Sarah at the gate and thought that's all I had to do. Mum completely forgot to steer and tell me we weren't finished so we over shot the jump a little. Now if she would just tell me where we were going we'd be fine but she seems so panicky about my ability to jump that she doesn't do her job. Leave me to do the jumping woman – you just point me in the right direction. Fence 5 then was red and black with this scary looking boy and a dog in red and black striped jumpers. I decided that the ice-cream van looked much more attractive so headed that way instead. Mum suggested my natural mother may not have been married to my father, dug her legs into me and made me jump it. Well if you want to get eaten by knasher – on your own head be it mother!

Mother managed to point me at the right jumps for a few more and despite us having a slight argument over the choice of gait between fences we did ok. I fail to see why I can't canter round the jumps – if Mum is having steerage issues this is not my fault.

Nor is it my fault that she ripped the front of her jodhpurs and so was showing all the Dads in the crowd her black frilly knickers. She calls ME embarrassing? I'm the one that looks like I am taking my special needs mother out for the day. Mind you it did look like she made a few of the old duffers days – it was perhaps the first time they'd seen frilly pants in years.

We managed to get round and Mum seemed pleased. I just wanted her to change her trousers before anyone else saw her underwear. When Aunty Sarah tactfully pointed it out she did look very embarrassed but it was a bit late by then. Mothers sometimes should not be let out on their own........

Anyway back to the happy hen farm place. Does anyone know where there are such places for horses? I really Fancy me and 1000 mares. They might kill me but heh I'd die happy.......

04.06.2010

Dear Diary
I am alarmed. I have known for some time that my mother is slowly but surely losing her marbles but it appears to be catching. Now I fear that she has passed dippyitus onto Evil Army Man and we are all now DOOMED.

I shall explain......

On Saturday it was raining, so of course muggins here is expected to work in it. Imagine my delight when therefore I saw Evil Army Mans car coming down the drive. I don't mind getting wet if we're going to do some jumping! Evil Army Mans mare came with him and his foal. The foal is quite sweet and seems to like me, which is of course understandable, but someone ought to tell the little dude that blowing snot bubbles is not a good look.

Anyway Mum tacked up and off we went. EAM got the jump wings out and said Mum was riding great – yada yada. I'm doing the work matey so I deserve the praise – Mum just sits there and tries to look intelligent.

We rode round whilst EAM and Dad set all the wings out, got the poles out and put the poles on the floor between the wings. On the floor? What's with that? This is why I think EAM has caught Mums dippyness. Surely to jump the poles have to be in the air? Come on, I know I'm a bog trotter but even I know what jump means. Show jumping – the clue is in the title people. You have to JUMP over poles. If it were called Show Stepping I would understand what we were playing at, but unless they have changed the rules without telling me then I just don't get it.

EAM said it didn't matter about the poles as we all know I can jump and the purpose of the exercise was for Mum to practise her bit – i.e. the turns. Now hang on a minute! Just because Mum is a spatially unaware Muppet how come that means I have to charge about in the rain, between jump wings but don't get to actually do the fun bit – i.e. the JUMPING?

Anyway we seemed to pass show stepping 101 as EAM seemed very pleased. I was not pleased and sulked for the rest of the day but no one seemed to notice. I have seriously got to learn how to throw an impressive hissy fit – apparently standing behind EAM yawning when he talks about the importance of good turns is too subtle. Damn....

On Sunday I helped Mum poo pick our fields – which she really appreciated. Fancy pants and I are still together in the same field but separated by electric tape as he was getting too "clingy" with me. I'm not sure what "clingy" is exactly but I do know he screams like a girl the minute I move. He's seriously uncool and killing any chance I might have had with the ladies.

On Sunday afternoon Mum and Dad decided to introduce me to the tractor that was parked at the yard. This was in order to "desensitise" me to tractors. Now I admit I don't like the things – they are loud, smelly and usually creep up on me when I'm out with Dad on my own. But if treats are on offer I can stand next to anything for a few minutes. Heh I'll even eat treats off its wheels. I am not fussed. Why Mum and Dad seemed so pleased with this I have no idea – I'll still not be happy when one is up my bum on a narrow back lane with no wing man for protection......

Anyway till next week. I'm off to see if I can entice Fancy pants to lean over the tape again – watching him jump 6 ft in the air when it bites him is hilarious!

11.06.2010

Dear Diary

This week I have moved further from the dog house and more towards the horse Hilton. This week I have been a good boy. I know this because mother keeps repeating it as if I didn't hear her the first time round. I am many things Mum but deaf isn't one of them.

Last weekend it was very hot so Mum decided that I could do some work on the lunge instead. This is roughly translated as she didn't want to get hot and sweaty but it was ok for me to. Needless to say with a small amount of martyred sighing I did everything she asked for, executed some lovely transitions up and down the gears (even if I do say so myself!) and generally behaved. She seemed rather pleased with all of that so I was happy.

Dad took me out on Tuesday for a hack with Fancy pants and despite him walking slow enough for his feet to set into the road we had a nice time.

Then yesterday Mum and Dad said I was having an "MOT". I had no idea what this meant but was soon to find out. First the nice German man came up to me in the field, gave me a cuddle and then walloped a great big needle in my neck. One of these days I am going to stop falling for that old chestnut….

Then Evil Army Man arrived. I thought it was odd as Mum didn't have her riding clothes on and he was wearing a rather camp all in one jumpsuit number - but going on the fact he has nuzzled me a few times (and I am very broad minded) I didn't think much of this. It was only when he produced his buckets of torture implements my thoughts of a fun afternoon jumping finally vanished.

This time apparently he was so sure I am a brave boy he decided to use power tools. What this meant is having a large drill stuck in my mouth and switched ON!! I have seen people drill holes in WALLS with drills! Anyway what with Mum cooing "good boy" and EAM having a vice like grip on my head collar, we managed to get through the experience without my pointing out to EAM what I really thought by planting my shoe up his nose. I have to admit it was over a lot faster than normal but still I'm not sure I'm keen on this power tool idea. What with that and his head torch on EAM is starting to look like some sort of insane professor. Remind me to keep a close eye on him – if he steals any of my hair etc I'll know for sure he has flipped and is creating Franken horse in the back barn. He did however say what a good boy I was so Mum was chuffed. What me being good has to do with her skills as a horse owner I have no idea, but hey Mum in a good mood = treats and a neck scratch so all is good.

This morning I went out with Mum for a hack, the first one we have been on together in ages. We went with big Billy from the stable next to me. He is HUGE! And quite brave so I decided to man up and not throw a complete abdab at every tractor that came by. Admittedly three pigeons doing a below radar fly by out of the hedge did make me jump which was rather uncool but I don't think he noticed. I did manage not to embarrass myself in front of the cement lorry and the crop sprayer so all was good. We even had a trot and things which is most unlike Mum so I think she's been taking some of that confidence stuff again - which is cool because I swear I heard her ask EAM for an XC lesson soon. Yippee!

Anyway I am off to lap up the attention of being "the bestest pony ever" (whatever that means?) for a while longer. Laters.....

18.06.2010

Dear Diary

I have exciting news! Mum has bought me a really cool present......... she's bought me my own lorry! She doesn't think I know about it but I saw it the other day. It's big and says "Hovis" down the side. Fancy pants says I'm being thick and that it was a bread lorry but I know what I saw! How cool am I? Having a lorry with my name on it. I can't wait to get in it but Mum is showing no signs of fetching it yet – perhaps it is a big surprise?

After last weeks trauma of having my yearly needle AND the dentist all in one day I've had quite a quiet one this week. Dad has been working so boss lady Sarah has been turning us out in a morning. This means strictly bestest behaviour as although she is only small she is very strict. Plus she prefers Fancy pants to me. That said she did say to Mum that I was a lovely stamp of a horse the other day. This amused Fancy pants who suggested Mum was going to lick me then post me to someone else. The boy may be pretty but clever he isn't.

Mum came back last night and poo picked the field which I helped with. Then I noticed that Tom and a few of the others were all running about like big scaredy cats. I couldn't figure out why until I saw this big spray of water come over the top of the barn. It was fab! It made rainbows and everything. Plus it went "whoosh whoosh" and tried to catch the humans out by pretending to have turned away then spraying them when they weren't looking! Boss lady Sarah seemed very upset and seemed to be calling the tractor men "idiots". Apparently the big spraying thing moves up and down the field watering the plants but it's not supposed to come down our end at the time when we're all coming in. I wasn't bothered – the spray was actually quite refreshing – so to show how manly I am Mum brought me in at the same time as pushing the poo barrow. I am so hard I make Chuck Norris look like a pansy. Talking of pansies, Fancy pants had his usual heart attack being made to come past something that might bite him. Mind you he was being a big Poof this morning with Mum just because someone was scaring birds off their crops. He is so uncool and I worry it ruins my reputation.

I was hoping to go out for a hack with Billy again today but Cool New Shoes Man came to give me some cool new shoes. I am worried about him. I think he is in need of a clip – he has much facial hair and I'm sure he shouldn't have. Heck Mum even shaves off my moustache so I'm sure his human mare must not like his new look. He looks like a bush on legs. Most peculiar. That said he found the spot in my neck that I love being scratched on today so all attempts at not being associated with him failed miserably as I waved about like Stevie Wonder on speed. Damn the man!

Anyway I'm off to catch up on munching before Mum comes back. I have a bad feeling she mentioned the "work" word earlier……..

25.06.2010

Dear Diary
My mother is trying to kill me. Its official, she doesn't love me any more and is trying to end my young life. How I hear you ask, have I come to this conclusion? Well simples. Last night she made me work for 40 MINUTES in 100 degree heat and today she had a lesson with Evil Army Man and he made us work for an HOUR in 100 degree heat. I was so wet with sweat by the time I'd finished that I looked like I'd just stepped out of the shower. SO not a good look.

EAM arrived this morning and tacked Fancy pants up – this surprised me but amused me no end. At last Fancy pants was going to know what its like to have EAM give you the thrashing of your wee small life. Alas no. Fancy pants got to do jumping which I have to say the dude is amazing at. I could probably run under the size jumps he and EAM were popping over. Damn him! He was nearly on his knees when they'd finished mind and he had sweat on his eyebrows! Yuck! Dude that is SO wrong. Even I don't sweat on my eyebrows and I'm a big hunk of sweaty feathered muscled mass when I finish. There is talk of him being too talented for Dad and sending him to someone who wants to compete at a serious level. How come? Mum and I compete very seriously – she seriously trys and I'm seriously embarrassed jumping against ponies………..

Anyway after Mum had dealt with the sweaty mess that used to be Fancy pants it was my turn. Mum caught me and EAM having a "moment" together and suggested that EAM might not be as evil as he thinks. I think this set him a challenge so we had an hour of "correct leg, right tempo, precise number of strides, precise take off point, perfect straightness" jumping. Yada yada yada. As long as I get over it does it matter? That said I do love jumping and is SO beat the 40 minutes of poncing about last night with my head in the right place whilst wilting in the 100 degree heat. Did I mention it's hot at the minute?

EAM said he's very proud of Mum and me and that we're turning into a good team. By this time I couldn't care less – I just wanted a cold shower and there was a queue. I wanted to get in the shower but I was not playing find the soap with Barney (he and Fancy pants get on well so enough said) so I had to wait.

The good news is at least Fancy pants and I both know we've got the rest of the day off as I don't think either Dad or Mum is nasty enough to make us work again. I think Mum said we might go out for a hack tomorrow and that she was going to take me for a play on the XC course but the ground is too hard. I'm hoping for an easy weekend – chilling out and watching the girls roll about trying to get cool – phwoarh!

Oh and before I go – my lorry still hasn't arrived yet. Is there a gift giving time coming up soon that Mum might be saving it for?

02.07.2010

Dear Diary

I am back in the dog house, Fancy pants and I are once again co-habiting with Fido. I blame Fancy pants myself but mother does not appear to share my view....

It started the other week when Mum announced that sun cream alone was not enough to keep my delicate little nose from burning and so produced the dreaded full face mask. I wore it last year and I didn't like it. This year I like it even less, mainly due to comments that were made by Dollys' Mum. Apparently I look like Darth Vador. Now at first I thought this sounded cool until someone told me that Darth Vador is an evil dude who kills little bear creatures and sounds like he has a frog in his throat. Either that or is in serious need of a Halls.....

Now pardon me for being a bit sensitive but I'm not being cast as anyone's baddy besides which I'll be damned if I'm going to sound like a dirty phone call so I decided I don't want to wear my mask. Thus every day I walk over to Pride and he takes it off for me. Simples. Except the other day he was a bit rough and has cut all my face - I don't mind but Mum is livid. She yesterday mentioned some dude called Gaffer Tape will make my mask stay on - not being funny but the guy had better be seriously bigger than me or I'm going to unleash a can of whoop ass on him if he tries.

On another note Pride might be going to a new home with someone EAM knows so that he can do BSJA. I didn't know what BSJA was so asked Billy. Apparently it stands for Big Scary Jumps Ahead so I don't envy him that! I will keep you posted.

Billy and I have been out for a nice hack today and Mum did lots more trotting so I think that confidence stuff is good. I even managed to not look a big Poof in front of Billy by walking past a big hissing thing which was spitting, several tractors and big lorries. Billy freaked at a bunch of purple flowers so I was most amused. I was not when we got home though as the big dude stood to one side and said "ladies first", in response I bit him and Mum hit ME!! How does that work? He started it!

Anyway I am now in the field chilling and watching some party that's going on at the house at the back of the yard. As we came back down the drive they were putting some of those floating coloured things on the gates. Billy wasn't keen on them either but I have seen them before so was cool. Sometimes ladies I AM the man! Laters

12.07.2010

Dear Diary

I apologise for not writing on Friday but Mum was up in Yorkshire with my older brother so I couldn't get to the computer. More on that in a minute. Well this week has been a tad quiet. This is because on Saturday Mum managed to lame herself in spectacular style by taking a swan dive off the lorry. It pains me to say but it wasn't even my or Fancy pants fault. My Mum is a plonker who fell over her own feet. Special needs I tell you......

Anyway Aunty Sarah looked after me on Saturday morning whilst Mum was at horsepital and then Dad rode me on Sunday whilst Mum stayed at home no doubt moaning about how much her ankle hurts.

She has come up every night to see me but she can't ride me. This task has fallen to Dad who does keep insisting on taking me out on my own with no wing men. On

Sunday we were nearly attacked by one of the big hissing spitting things but yet again my swift reactions saved us from certain doom. I'm not sure Dad saw it this way as much muttering about "wimpy bog trotter" was going on but I assumed he was referring to someone else? "Wimpy" and my name never feature in the same sentence together…….

On Friday Mum and Aunty Sarah came up and got the lorry out – yippee thought I - we're going out! Alas no. Mum was going with Aunty Sarah to fetch my older brother who is retired in York and take him to the vets. After he injured himself several years ago he has been chilling out and relaxing, but Mum and Dad felt it was time to have another x-ray on his badly damaged foot to see how bad its got. I really wanted to go and see him but Mum said that Sid didn't like me then and was unlikely to like me now so I wasn't allowed. She's such a spoil sport.

Apparently Mum was really worried about him loading as he's not been near a lorry in 2 years but he went straight on. Then he threw an absolute fit on the lorry so Mum and Aunty Sarah had to load his best mate the donkey on with him to keep him calm. Now why is it all my brothers have been big girls blouses? And seriously dude what's with the donkey? Apparently Mum and Aunty Sarah felt like a right bunch of gypsies turning up at the vets with a strapping 17.2HH Hanoverian and his donkey side kick. Oh and Mum with a walking stick and Aunty Sarah's trousers falling down flashing her cow pants at the vets during the trot up. I was SO glad I didn't go when I heard all this. I love my Mum and Aunty Sarah but there are times when I think they shouldn't be let out on their own.

Anyway the upshot is Sids foot is very very bad on the x-ray but he's actually not that lame. His injury is so special they asked Mum if they can use his x-rays for teaching purposes. His field mates will never hear the end of that I can tell you. So Sid has gone back to his field and will see the vet in a year. I suppose that means I'd better get saving for his Christmas present. So in the meantime Mum is still on box rest and bute and is very very fed up. Do you think I should lend her my treat ball?

16.07.10

Dear Diary
Fancy Pants has left the building! He is away on trial – trial for what I'm not sure? Crimes against masculine geldings by being a big girls blouse? Mum says it's so he can be assessed. I could have done that for them and saved the trouble:

Is he a horse? Yes tick.

Does he have four legs? Yes, tick.

Can he jump very big fences? Damn his eyes, yes, tick.

Is he an utter Poof, frightened of his own shadow who screams like a girl? Oh definitely yes, tick.

There you go, job done. In summary he is a talented dipstick who is a prancing pansy. Simples.

Mum said he shouted for me the whole journey to his new yard – what a pansy. I don't do shouting and creating, I am the strong silent type, although I did let myself down this morning and whinny to Mum. Ooops.

Anyway Mum is still lame so Dad had been riding me. We've been out hacking on our own – what is it with Dad and this flying solo business? I much prefer going with someone else as I can leap behind them if required but Dad says I have to learn to be brave and go by myself. Seriously I don't think I do.

Then Mum mentioned that Dad might be taking me to a show tomorrow so last night we practised jumping. Now Dad has funny ideas about hacking but I much prefer his ideas about jumping. I am therefore hoping that tomorrow is an actual SHOW and not another jumping over trotting poles competing against small children and ponies the size of dogs – i.e. Mums idea of a show. Apparently it is at the place that Mum flashed her knickers at everyone so I am hoping this time she manages to keep her underwear choices between her and Dad and not share them with every person in the crowd.

So last night Dad and I jumped over some fences whilst Mum shouted encouragement. I'm not sure who all the "good boy", "clever boy" was aimed at – me or Dad – but either way both of us ignored her. Dad has the same yeehaa approach to jumping that I have, so what we lack in style, finesse, and talent we make up for in thundering enthusiasm and boing-boing-ability.

We'll probably flatten every fence there but heh it'll be fun. I'm hoping this time Dad might get the hint when I kick as we go past that happy hen place. I so want to at least try the idea of 1,000 happy mares and 3 ecstatic geldings. So ladies – mass HHO horse meet up at mine this weekend? You bring yourselves I'll supply the hay and the lurve. What do you say?

23.07.2010

Dear Diary

I do not know what I have done to my father. I try to be a good boy, not tread on his toes, try not to laugh when he gets bitten by the biting fence and what do I get in return? Nearly killed that's what. But more on that in a minute.

As I told you last week Dad took me jumping on Saturday back to the place where Mum likes to flash her knickers. Thankfully she managed to keep her underwear under wraps this time and Dad and I were left to do some jumping. Now the course is on grass and quite spread out which I like as it means I can get a lot of speed up between jumps. And I do mean a LOT. This didn't go down well with Dad, who unlike Mum does like to canter courses - just it appears not at warp speed. Three rounds later I think he'd finally come around to my way of thinking and was letting me get on with my job. Well either that or he was too exhausted to fight with me anymore? Either way we did ok but I didn't make the jump off – Mum said I only kissed the pole that fell. This is incorrect as I kicked it with my foot and last time I kissed something I swear it involved tongues? Mum is strange…..

On the way home we had a drama as there was a big dog running about in the road. Because my Mum and Dad are so nice they parked the horse box in the middle of the road and went after the dog. Excuse me?! How is it ok to use me and my executive accommodation to stop oncoming traffic? Anyway Mum caught the dog and it turned out to be one of the doggies that chase foxes. They'd been out exercising and he'd got left behind. Ooops. Anyway Mum and Dad got him back to where he lived so that all ended well.

I had the day off on Sunday to recover – more likely for Dads arms to go back to normal length. Then on Monday Dad and I went for a hack – on our own……..again. But this time he truly tried to kill me. We went the route where we have to cross the metal snakes lair TWICE! At the first crossing all was well although I swear I saw Mum in her car at the side of the road? Then we cut across a big field towards the other end of the lair. We were just coming to the end of the field when a metal insect came towards us! It was like a big yellow metal spider! It had huge arms and I swear fangs, it had certainly already eaten a man as I could see him in its belly………. I tried to get us away but Dad was obviously in the mood to die so made me go past it. Apparently this breed is called a crop sprayer and isn't dangerous – yeeaah RIGHT! Tell that to the bloke it had eaten! Then as we approached the second crossing there was a beeping noise and the gates to the snakes home shut. What happened next was so traumatic I will have nightmares for weeks. TWO great big snakes went past, then a big red Hovis eating tractor snuck up behind us and three smiling assassins on those bike things joined it. It was terrifying. Dad kept insisting that I had to stay where I was and I can tell you I was not keen on that idea AT ALL. Then as the snakes lair opened again a BUS came the other way! By this time I was seriously thinking of jumping into Mums car with her and demanding a lift home. I can man up with the best of them but this was utter madness! If it was a test of my toughness I submit. Call me a pansy and dress me in dresses but don't make me do that again. EVER. Then as we got past all these horrible things the big spraying thing in the field wee'd on me......... By this stage I was so stressed I didn't really care but the indignity of it will stay with me for life. Not that my life will be very much longer if Dad has his way. He is a LOON. Mum please get sound soon – you may be weird but at least I don't think you want to finish me off.

Then yesterday to confirm his desire to kill me Dad took me in the school in 200 degree heat and made me do TRANSITIONS. Lots and lots and lots and lots of them. Even walk to canter. When I didn't do it really quick he hit me on the bum with a whip! Now I'm sorry but for a big boy like me it takes some effort to switch from front wheel to rear wheel drive so less of the whip father dearest. Mind you Mum wasn't much better – she reckons that someone called Carl Nester says you should do 100 transitions per schooling session. Great my mother is taking riding advice from big bird....... I am DOOMED

30.07.2010

Dear Diary
Its been 7 months since the love of my life was tragically put to sleep on Christmas eve. I have looked at other ladies and perhaps even felt a stirring of lust for a few but none have really taken my Fancy. Well I think my heart may be mending....... More on that in a moment.

This week as Mum is still lame Dad has taken me out. This week we have been out alone and then we went out with Dolly. She's quite cute but older than me and a bit high maintenance. I don't think she liked the fact that I had molasses all over my nose from the yummy yummy lickit Mum and Dad got me the other day. Dad said it made me look even more like a spikey pony than normal – I'm not sure how much I normally look like one so I didn't get it. What is a spikey? Is it like those little dudes with the bad hair cuts that I see scuttling about at night?

Anyway Dollys Mum wanted to make sure I behaved before she would let Dolly come out with me to go fast so we walked.........everywhere. YAWN. I'm sure my standing in the neighbourhood went up by being seen out with a lovely lady (rather than a bunch of chunky men) but still I'm far happier when we get to hurtle about the countryside like feathered Ferraris - alas not this time. I did try to behave myself so maybe Dollys Mum will let us run next time.

The other night Dad gave me a shave and tried to scrub the molasses off my nose so Mum wouldn't see me looking like such a tramp. I don't think Mum can say anything about being a tramp – she went to the supermarket the other day wearing the hay on her head and my dinner down her back, how that all got there I have NO idea……..

Then last night SHE arrived. Hubba Hubba. I don't even know her name yet but I walked into the barn and there she was - opposite my stable. Her ears went up and she neighed "hey big boy" – well in my head she did I couldn't understand a word of it. Mum thinks she might be welsh so perhaps that explains it. Despite the language barrier she is HOT. I LIKE. Best of all only she and I came in last night so I had all night to prance about looking manly. She was impressed I could tell but I really wish Mum wouldn't stand there killing herself laughing. I do NOT look like a peacock I look like a stallion. Mum needs to get her wildlife books out – seriously she was ruining it all. I am trying to think of some good lines to entice her but Mum says "How would you like to be wrapped in a hunk of Hovis" makes it sound like I want to turn her into a horseburger. Any ideas on some better ones?

Best of all they are cutting the field around us which only means one thing – stubble! A fit lady, stubble fields and molasses. Boy its been a good week………….

06.08.2010

Dear Diary

This week has been lovely and relaxing. Yes that's right – my mother wasn't here! She and Dad were away so the boss lady has been looking after me. This I like for several reasons: a) she doesn't work me, b) she grooms me every day without moaning at my questionable parentage and lack of polish and c) she feeds me loads more than Mum does. All of these things are good!

Better still I have been making serious inroads with my new lady friend. As reported last week this fine looking filly turned up unexpectedly last week. She was put in the field at the end of the ménage and to my horror the old dude Tom was put next to her to keep her company. Now I'm sorry I admire my elders and all that but back off buddy I saw her first. Luckily it seemed she didn't like him and he didn't like her and so spent the time stressing, yelling loudly and generally acting like a fairy. I then over heard Mum say to boss lady that if Tom didn't settle that she could use me to baby sit the new girl. There are times when I love my mother more than life itself. Genius! "Baby sit" – Ha! I love it! Anyway boss lady took Mum up on her offer and thus I was moved to be next to the girl in question, who I now know is called Smartie and is rather tarty...... just the way I like them!

So I have spent the week canoodling. Yum yum. I like Smarties! My moves were nearly ruined when a new dude turned up and was put into a tiny fenced off bit next to us but Smartie is not interested. What a girl! Alas it appears ours is only going to be a summer romance as she is just on loan to the lady who owns the dude in the small paddock. In summary he's going off to be schooled and Smartie is here in the meantime. Never mind I've never had a holiday romance so I'm making the most of it. Apparently my manly good looks have brought her into season. I'm not entirely sure what that means but the girl is so full on she's scaring me a bit! (Not that I'm telling her that). Something tells me she's a girl of some experience so I'm happy to let her be my Mrs Robinson for the summer.

In other news mother is now off box rest and rode me last night. I don't know if the amount of swearing going on was due to a sudden onset of tourettes or if it hurt quite a lot. Either way Mum once again expressed her vast vocabulary quite loudly.

Today a man came to look at my saddle and to my delight has taken it away. Yippee no work for me! Alas I swear I heard Mum mention that pissola thing so I may not be getting off scot free. She says I have to start using my bum more than my shoulders? Why? I have big manly shoulders and I don't want a big bum. Don't get me wrong I love big butts and I cannot lie (do you like that? I should be a song writer.....). Just I like them on girls not on me. Anyone else think this is all wrong?

13.08.2010

Dear Diary
I am doomed. After a week lazing in the field, eating, chillaxing and generally having fun Mother returned yesterday. With her came the saddle man with my saddle. Poo. I seriously was hoping for at least another week or so of no work but alas mother seems to have other ideas.

After saddle man had finished poking me and the saddle which way and that way mother leapt aboard (ok scrambled in a slightly inelegant fashion – sorry Mum I have to be honest and Ellen Whitaker you aren't) and proceeded to play about in the ménage whilst proclaiming the saddle felt much better. I have to say I didn't notice much difference other than mother may have been on double hay rations last week……….not that I was brave enough to mention this.

So today the dawn came and along with it black clouds, howling winds and much general nastiness. I prepared myself for a day grazing in the shelter of the big hedge when Mum turns up with my saddle. Has she gone stark raving insane? Then Billys Mum arrived with his tack and the awful truth dawned upon me – we were going for a hack. Now I love hacking but hacking in a monsoon is not my idea of fun. Plus I have noted of late an increase in the number of the tractors of terror. Is it their breeding season? Mother and Aunty C proudly announced they were not fair weather riders. Maybe not Mum but I am fast seeing the attraction of being a fair weather horse…

Anyway despite me playing her up in the stable to the extent she smacked me on the shoulder with a brush, mother insisted on dragging me out and making me follow Billy. Well let me tell you I know its Friday the 13th but was there any need to send 8 tractors out after us? There was one that came towards us offering a big bale of straw in its claws like a bribe - "Come eat my straw my prettys". Yeah right then you'll leap on us and before we know it we'll have our legs wrapped round our heads as Billy and Hovis bales. No thank you. We survived the encounters but Mum seemed to find my manly snorting funny and called me a pansy. Moi? Pansy? I think she's got me confused with someone else. Admittedly I did prance like Darcy Bussell over that weird red road with the 30 sign on it but heh a boy can't be too careful – road shouldn't be red. Its in the rules. Plus we all know that for sale signs eat horses so why Mum has not been appraised of this yet I have no idea. The woman is so behind the times..

Anyway we went for a nice trot and Mum mentioned something about stubble racing but the big spraying thing was going in the field next door and Mum and Aunty C said they weren't going to tempt fate. Who's fate? Is she fit? And do you tempt her with a carrot or a mint?

Eventually we got back home and Mum put me out in the field. We've had a change around of late so I'm no longer next to tarty Smartie. This is ruining my chances of a summer romance with my equine Mrs Robinson and I think is unjustly unfair. Could one of you tell Mum to move me back so I can pull please? I'm next to big bad Billy now and the dude is cool but not exactly as much fun as tarty Smartie. Thankfully he does seem to be a mans man and thus has not attempted to give me any hugs from behind. This makes him alright in my book but I need to get back to the ladies. I need a cunning plan – any suggestions?

20.08.2010

Dear Diary

I've had quite a good week this week as Mum had to work away for 4 days rather than 3 so its been very relaxing.

Mind you I needed that time to recover from the weekend. Since Mum works away she insists that the days she's home we HAVE to work, no mater what the weather or anything. So on Friday (as reported last week) I was made to endure a hack of trek like endurance with howling wind and rain. Oh and tractors – lots of tractors.

On Saturday she made me work in the ménage on our turns. YAWN. Now ok I do admit when I get excited out jumping some of my turns can be a little unorthodox but that's not reason to make me endure an hour of boring circles, transitions and general ponciness. If I promise to stop cornering like a very large, hairy Valentino Rossi do you think she'll stop? Its so dull. The only highlight was the fact tarty Smartie is in a field near the ménage so it was like a nice merry-go-round…hello-yummy-Smartie-more-dull-trotting-hello-yummy-Smartie-more-dull-trotting-hello-yummy-Smartie-more-dull-trotting…….. you get the idea. She got bored watching so have a little bit of sympathy for how boring I found it all.

Then on Sunday Mum returned to the idea that I need to ponce about like a giant fairy with my head on my chest. Damn it all I thought she'd given up on that particular daft idea. We had a few brief moment of arguing about this before she reminded me who is boss…..well more to the point reminded me she carries a schooling whip and it stings.

Still apparently I was not behaving well enough so Dad got on. "Hurrah!" Thought I "Yeehaa cantering and no cares about nicely cornering or poncy head carriage". But no! I think my Dad has had an epiphanny, epifenny, epif - damn it I am only a horse I can't spell that – a brain fart, because he insisted on me poncing about also. This is SO not on. Do I look like a dressage diva? I sulked for the rest of the day until Mum gave me carrots, then I lost my ability to strop as its uncool to do so with a mouth full of orangey goodness.

Anyway for the rest of this week Billy and I have been hanging out in the fields behind the hedge. Mum says we have been put behind the hedge because we lower the tone of the place and that way boss lady Sarah gets to hide the two bog monsters from view. I think that is featherist and I demand to be treated equally to the sleek, free-from-sawdust-in-their-manes-and-tails-but-nonetheless-wimpy TBs on the yard. That said we have the place to ourselves and so have had a boys week chilling out and eating lots of good grass.

Mum is coming back later to ride and is already threatening dire consequences if I am naughty. I have tried to point out its raining and blowing a gale but Mother will not be deterred………….. someone call me the men with the white coats……….

27.08.2010

Dear Diary

Well what a week! This week marked a serious milestone in Mum and I's life together – this week after 3 years we finally went stubble racing together! I've been stubble racing loads with Dad and Aunty Sarah but Mum has never taken me. She's often said how much she wanted to but she's never been brave enough – I don't know why? I am big and brave and am not naughty so I'm not sure what she has been scared of? Maybe she is allergic to stubble?

Anyway on Sunday we saddled up to go out for a hack with Billy and Billy's Mum, as we walked off the yard Billy's Mum asked my Mum where she fancied going and Mum replied " somewhere with stubble fields so we can have a run"!!!!! I was so surprised I nearly fell over and kissed Billy's bottom (which is totally unmanly so I managed to regain my footing pretty quick).

Anyway off we toddled and found a big field which belongs to boss lady Sarah. Mum made me trot across the first bit which I did very nicely because I knew what was coming next! Then Mum asked me for canter and we were off!! Mum and Billy's Mum had spent lots of time making plans for if I got silly and what to do etc but hadn't made plans for the fact I am turbo charged (and in fairness Billy's junior by nearly a factor of 3!!). We went off and left Billy in our wake! Yeehaa!! I could hear Mum yelling yeehaa in my ear so I went even faster. She wasn't asking me to go as fast as Dad usually asks but we were motoring! The one thing that made me sad was that Fit mare was not next to me. She was the only one who has ever been able to keep up and was always my stubble racing partner. I swear I could sense her with me though, those long black legs of hers matching me stride for stride. It was as if she was by my shoulder as we charged across the field. At the end Mum pulled me up and then flung her arms round my neck yelling with happiness. It was fab! We then waited for Billy to catch up and then pootled through the village where I surprised a man by putting my head through his car window when he stopped to admire us. Well he said I was handsome so I thought he might like a closer look? Mum luckily was in such a good mood she found it funny. We then walked and trotted across another two stubble fields although I did fancy another run. The only blot on my impeccable copy book was as we neared home two horses appeared in front of us and started trotting away from us. I fancied going and having a chin wag with them and Mum and I did have a little disagreement over this. In the end we went a different way home with mother reminding me in her stern tone that she was the boss. Yeah right – whatever makes you feel better Mum!

Last night I had another one of those talks from her as I tried to join in a fight that was going on whilst she was leading me to the stables. Apparently behaving like a Spanish riding school horse is not acceptable behaviour when Mum is on the other end of the lead rope and so 30 minutes of reminding me of my manners in the school swiftly followed. Needless to say this morning I walked out like a lamb – that lead rope stings!

Tonight Mum tells me I am going to a clinic. I'm not sure why as I am not ill but she did mention Evil Army Man is going to be there - I'm hoping this means jumping but I'm not sure how we jump in a clinic? Is it like hospital bed hurdles or something? Would someone please explain?

PS Mum is going away for a few weeks so there will be no diaries until she gets back. She's said boss lady Sarah can ride me whilst she's away so I may have much to tell you!

17.09.2010

Dear Diary
It has been two weeks since my last confession – I mean entry – so I have much to tell you.

As you may recall on the day of my last entry I was informed by Mum that I was going to a clinic. No ladies – not that kind of clinic, a JUMPING clinic. Excitedly I thought this may entail chasing fit nurses over hospital bed hurdles but alas not. It meant a group of us being beasted by Evil Army Man.

Upon arriving I was delighted to see lots of lovely ladies but they seemed to all look down their fine pedigree noses at me which I thought was rude. Admittedly Mum hadn't had time to wash my feathers but still books and covers ladies, books and covers. They all looked fractionally more interested when some of my fans arrived and asked if I was indeed THE Hovis. Is there any other?!

Anyway we got on with the task in hand and soon started showing the others how its done. Well I think that's what Dad was getting excited about (he was riding as Mum had been to the person who fixes ankles that morning), either that or he was being picky about being on the right leg again. We got to jump lots of jumps in a big arena which was good fun and at the end we did a full course – which I of course jumped clear. Evil Army Man said to the others that they should not be deceived by my feathers and manly muscles – underneath it all was a jumping machine. Still this did not seem to impress these posh SJ-ing mares so I went home alone. The next day Mum and Dad went on holiday and left me in the capable hands of boss lady Sarah. She is small, quite bossy and I don't dare put a foot wrong in her presence. Mum also said she could ride me so I was put through my paces. She may be small but that woman has legs of iron! And is SO fussy about little things like the correct lead and bend and flex and all sorts. Sheesh! I've never sweated so hard since my beloved was alive and flashed her studs at me once. That said we did go on some nice hacks with Billy and his Mum, and boss lady is braver than Mum so lots of cantering!

Anyway time flew by and Mum and Dad came back. They tried to appease me of the fact they'd left me being beasted by bossy-correct-lead-lady by bringing me some Spanish horse treats. The Spanish people don't like their horses much do they? YUCK! So Mum bought me some carrots instead – much nicer. This morning Mum and I have had a nice little ride in which Mum appeared to be ecstatic that I cantered each time on the right leg. Damn right mother – you'll turn me back over to Mrs Iron legs otherwise and I much prefer your short fat stumpy ones – they don't inflict as much squeezing!

I'm now off to laze in the sun and exchange notes with Billy about women, life and leg leads. Laters..........

24.09.2010

Dear Diary
I am sorry for the lateness of my entry today but Mum and Aunty C have been trying to kill Billy and I for most of the morning.

Despite hurricane like conditions, monsoon rains and a definite chill in the air, mother and Aunty C in their wisdom decided as they are not "fair weather riders" that we were still going out on our hack today. Admittedly this was agreed only after 20 minutes of "its up to you, I don't mind", "I don't mind, do you really want to go" which made it perfectly clear that really neither of them was keen but determined not to be the one that wussed out. I would have quite happily said I didn't want to go but sadly neither Billy nor I were given an option....

So Billy and I have endured two HOURS of slippery fields, driving rain, train lines, kamikaze ducks, lots of irrigators, tractors, postal vans, large green fuel dump things, blowing plastic bags and general mayhem so that mother and Aunty C could feel virtuous. Hah! We could have DIED, I fell over my feet at least 40 times and there's lots of deep ditches...

Seriously if its not a cruelty case I don't know what is.

This is AFTER mother made me school in the rain last night with God making loud noises and throwing light stick things at us. She did quit when the man upstairs started getting more accurate with the light stick things and they were getting a bit close. She said I was lethargic - nope Mum I'm just busy messing myself at the thought of being turned into a deep fried Hovis burger at any minute.

Earlier in the week Dad took me out hacking on our own (he's still not grown out of this silly habit) and worked me in the school. So all in all I think I've been put through it enough this week without having to endure Army style training in all weathers - Mum is spending too much time with Evil Army Man.

Talking of which his best friend, Cool New Shoes Man is coming later which means I'll be expected to stand on three legs for half the evening. Why he can't hold me up I have no idea but he's got very moany about me leaning on him. At least it means I can come in out of this horrible weather - the wind is playing havoc with the long mane I have now managed to grow. I am a little alarmed as I swear I heard Mum muttering something about mane pulling this weekend.

I also understand she has been on horse and hound online forum asking about cutting off my feathers? AND some of you told her to do it? I thought you were my friends? My fans? My lovely people? THEN you suggest she cuts off my feathers? What kind of people are you?!! Without my feathers I will look like a fat ginger bloke with bandy legs - how the heck am I supposed to pull looking like that? Sheesh a boy could go off you lot.........

01.10.2010

Dear Diary

I am concerned about Mum. I think she's been on that confidence stuff again – yesterday we went on the longest, scariest hack we've ever been on and she only started breathing funny once! Admittedly I was breathing funny too as we were sandwiched between two massive lorries on a very busy road and I was NOT happy.

Anyway I will start at the beginning….

Mum and Dad have been very busy with work so boss lady Sarah looked after me for the beginning of the week. This is always nice as I do no work, she gives me a lovely groom and lots of food!

Anyway Mum came back yesterday and as it was a nice day we decided to go out for a stroll with Billy and his Mum. I heard much discussion about where we were going and Billy's Mum asked my Mum if she was feeling brave. I nearly fell over when Mum said yes! So off we set and I soon realised I'd not got a clue where we were going – this always concerns me as Mum has no navigation skills at all and is likely to get us lost. Thus I stuck close to Billy, determined where ever he was going I was going too. This was a great idea until we got onto a stretch of nasty road where the people were very rude and kept driving very fast and close. Aunty C and Mum demonstrated their fluent grasp of the English language – all I can say is there are a LOT of people in Lincolnshire who didn't know who their Dads were…….

I was coping fine with all this until a very very large lorry parked on my feathers from behind. Now I'm a man so I'm not keen on things being close to me from behind anyway (I've never forgotten the incident with Fancy pants) and since Billy's bum was in front of me it forced me to make a rather camp move of nearly laying my head across his bottom in my attempt to save my feathers from being road kill.

THEN another big lorry came from the other way and heh presto we were lorry sandwich! Mum started breathing a bit funny and I was keen to get out of there post haste. Aunty C told the lorry behind us to wait a sec as she could spot a gap in the hedge for us to get into – but no the lorry knew best and continued to park on my bum. Now I know I have a lovely bum but it doesn't need examining in headlights two inches off my tail. We managed to trot on to the gap in the hedge where I proved I am not stupid by ensuring I squeezed into the gap in front of Billy.

Anyhow the horrible lorries left to go and do lorry things and we soon turned off onto a lovely long, car free bridleway. Here we had a nice trot and then a canter. The reason the canter wasn't lovely is that Mum made me go behind Billy and despite the mans athletic build he sure doesn't go that fast. I ended up doing a collected canter that would have made that Tortilla bloke proud (is he Mexican by the way? Why else name yourself after a crisp?). To make up for making me ponce about Mum let me go at the front for our second canter so I left Billy boy in my wake. He cheated at the end though because Mum pulled me up and he went two strides further than me thus getting back into the lead. Cheat!

The ride back was nice as the roads were very quiet winding country lanes with no traffic. There was a very scary lair at the side of the road – apparently its called a bus shelter but I think that's a code word because no bus I've seen could fit into it. We had a final hairy moment as close to home a tractor came and we had no where to get off the road so we trotted on a bit and then two men with a machine tried to ambush us from the side. I was impressed with Mums balance – a while back my athletic leap to save us may have unseated her.

I am most proud of Mum that she coped with all the scary things but this new found confidence is scary. What if she makes me do something really dangerous next? My young life could be cut off in its prime!

So Diary my conundrum for this week – how do I encourage Mum to do the fun things with me but dissuade her from getting us killed?

08.10.2010

Dear Diary

I am in the dog house. Mum is not happy with me at all. All was fine until this morning - I will explain more in a minute.

This week boss lady Sarah has looked after me for the beginning part of the week. This followed a weekend of Mum poncing me about the ménage - this apparently was due to being "inspired" by that Tortilla bloke. Now call me old fashioned but what some Mexican dude who calls himself after a Dorrito crisp has to do with me parading around our arena with my head on my chest I have NO idea. Apparently there have been some games on recently and lots of horses were invited. I took affront at this - why wasn't I invited? Was it some elitist warm blood party where hairy macho men like me weren't allowed in? I heard Mum telling Aunty C that some bloke called Fox-in-a-hole had done very well. Yeah well I bet he'd not win the apple bobbing games if I'd been there?

I got thinking about why I'd not been invited to this games party and concluded that you have to have a posh name to get on the guest list. That Moorlands Tortilla dude got in so this got me thinking........... I'd now like you all to call me "Boglands Quaver". I think it has a certain ring about it don't you? Thus newly named I have awaited my invite all week to these games but one has not turned up yet. Do you think its got lost in the post?

Whilst I waited for my invite I was grazing alone yesterday when this big machine started ploughing up the earth in the field next to me - needless to say I wasn't too happy about this and I admit got myself into a bit of a lather. Well more than a bit - I was more lathered than a poodle in a washing machine. So when Mum arrived she was very worried about me, sponged me down, got me lovely tasting water to drink and then spoilt it by giving me a tiny amount of tea. This was apparently in case I got colic. I've never seen anyone with this colic thing but I can tell you I don't fancy it much - boss lady Sarah came and poked me most of the night to check I was ok. By the third time of the lights going on at 11pm I was like "love, get over yourself, I know I'm cute but I'm also sleep deprived so can you stare at my manliness in the morning like civilised people?"

Anyway this morning Mum arrived, decided I was fine (like duh?! of course I'm fine - I AM Boglands Quaver) and off we tootled with Billy and his Mum. That's when I ended up in the casa del fido.......

We were having a very nice canter over some stubble fields, I had just over taken slow coach Billy and was pulling steadily away when a dive bomber attacked me low and fast from the hedge line. Like the seasoned warrior I am I threw myself left in a lightening move designed to save Mum and I's life. Except Mum lost a stirrup and shouted a LOT of rude words at me. Some people are SO ungrateful. I don't think the couple of seconds delay in her asking me to stop and me actually stopping helped either. Oooooopppps.

Anyway she let me trot most of the way home and berated me for being an idiot for most of the journey - how saving us from one of those low flying orange and green attack drones is idiotic I have no idea. I think Darwin's theory fails when it comes to my Mum.

Anyway she has put me in a new field next to Tom and that Ronny dude and gone home - no doubt discussing with people my bravery.
So till laters - I've got some grass eating to do

18.10.2010

Dear Diary
I am so sorry I didn't write on Friday but Mum was in Londonium so I could get access to the laptop. Not that it would have mattered if I did. I probably wouldn't have been able to get any signal from within the casa de pero which is where I am firmly residing at the moment.........

Last weekend Mum and Dad ruined my life. There I have said it.... they RUINED my life. I have been SHORN. Like a sheep! I have no fur, I look like a baby seal, all my manly gingerness has gone and been replaced by a delicate shade of pale grey which has had every other Mum on the yard making cooing noises about how "sweet" I look. I am not SWEET. I am the Destroyer. A big manly beast - not a cute sweet little thing - apparently I look about 4 years old again. The only good news is Mum fought off an attack by boss lady Sarah and Dad to take my legs off too so at least I still have my feathers.

Anyway my newly acquired streamlined look has got me in a world of trouble this week....

First of all I have been put in a new field with lots and lots of grass. My new field is next to Dolly who is the yard matriarch and until now she has paid about as much attention to me as road kill. That was until I managed to upend the bin that her Mum puts outside her field with "stuff" in it and empty said "stuff" all over the place. In the process I found a box of treats which was very nice. I also discovered Dollys Mum can run quite quickly and shout very loudly.......... ooooooppps....... Then on Thursday Mum got on me for a ride. Well I am sorry but I have had a week eating great grass, I am now no longer weighed down with fur - what exactly did she expect? Apparently my enthusiastic jumping into canter was inappropriate and resulted in me being lunged till I nearly died of exhaustion. I hate my life...

On Saturday we went to a jumping clinic and Dad rode me. This was partly due to Mum not wishing to fall off in front of some of her friends - which worked well as a tactic - Dad fell off instead.... Admittedly my last minute swerve to go and gawp at a fit chick parading up and down a nearby field probably didn't help matters but I refuse to take full responsibility for it. Dad should have held on tighter. I jumped everything else very well but that fence was far too close to a hottie and a boy cannot be blamed for wanting to do what bunnies do.

So Dads not happy with me, Mums not happy with me, Dollys Mum is not happy with me, all in all I am not in the good books.

On the plus side Dolly has come round far more since my new haircut and actually called out to me yesterday. She also ended up in trouble as she broke loose in the barn and sauntered down for a chat over my stable door the other night. I am thinking of playing hard to get but I think I am slightly too desperate to pull that off with any conviction. Maybe its my new "Boglands Quaver" posh name that has thawed her?

Talking of which Mum says the games are over now so I can go back to being just Hovis. I think it stinks that I was not invited. Mum says there's a big games party in 2012, I will be 9 by then so do you think I will be allowed to go?

22.10.2010

Dear Diary
Please can you arrange delivery of food rations and carrots to:
Casa del Fido
In deep doo doo lane
Smacked Bottom
Ooopshire
HE2 3LP

The reason for this request is simple - I think I'm going to be staying there for a while....
I was doing so well this week, after accidentally flattening Dad and very nearly EAM at last weeks jumping clinic I have made such an effort to regain my halo.
On Wednesday I didn't pass comment on being asked to do trotting poles for 30 minutes nor refuse to wind in and out of upturned buckets - although this did make me wonder once again about my mothers mental health?

Yesterday I cantered very nicely for Mum whilst we worked on correct strike offs and using the corners of the school to ensure we could execute good turns into jumps. I didn't even throw a hissy when Mum put the pole we were cantering over in the wrong place so I had to execute a turn Darcey Bussell would have been proud of just to get there.

So all in all Mum was happy with me, I was on bestest behaviour giving lots of cuddles and generally being my utterly adorable self.

Then this morning I let myself down - AGAIN. Dammit I wish I would learn but I just forget myself and then whoops I did it again I'm back residing with the pooch. We went out for a hack with Billy and Aunty C and had several nice trots down the country lanes in the sunshine saying hi to a few nice ladies and generally being Bad Boys out cruising the hood. Then we cut back across stubble fields and Mum and Aunty C decided to have a canter. Well I had been waiting for this like Rudolph waits for Christmas, I am feeling very well at the moment - I have lots of lovely grass, Dolly is fancying me, I have a new aerodynamic haircut, the sun is shining and all is right with the world. So its not my fault that when asked to step up a pace I leap forward to comply, put my head down (to achieve greater streamlinedness) and GO!!

Apparently mother doesn't see it that way and after I realised that we were no longer going in a straight line and the sound of the wind whistling past my ears was being interspersed by a voice yelling about my dodgy parentage I suspected all was not well. Admittedly it did take a while for any of this to register but when you are travelling at the speed of sound understanding what "whoa, you big fat, hair arsed git" means is somewhat tricky. I did pull up eventually to see what the noise was about and to suggest to mother that her circling me was silly as mach 5 is only achievable in a straight line. Something I tried to demonstrate when we tried to carry on in trot across the rest of the field....

I then was trotted all the way home whilst being informed of the many ways mother was planning on introducing me to my maker. Top of the list was feeding me through one of the carrot sorting machines on the farm - apparently she thinks Hovis batons and Hovis and Swede could be the new thing on the Sunday dinner table. Personally I think she may have got a bash on the head from one of her large girl saddle bags whilst we were running.....

Anyway the next cunning plan is to take me out for a canter on one of the tracks where they can wedge me behind Billy to force me to canter in an "appropriate manner" - AKA so slowly I look like a dressage Diva with a broom up my bum. What's wrong with warp speed? Mums been taking that confidence stuff, she likes going fast now so I was merely showing her where the turbo button is - I mean you don't own a Ferrari because its fuel economic and ditto you don't have a Destroyer to ponce. If I wanted to go slowly enough to count the blades of grass I'd WALK.

So here I reside in the dog house, shunned because of my amazing speed and power, punished for being living proof big boys can run at any time (not just when there's a half price sale at Carrots 4 U) and outcast for failing to understand that high speed questioning of who Dad was is not Mums idea of small talk. Life SUCKS.

PS Will someone please send me a carrot in the post as I doubt I'll be getting any for a while?

PPS Does anyone who likes going v v v v v v fast want to let me come and stay at theirs until Mum calms down?

29.10.2010

Dear Diary
I am leaving home. I have decided that I can't cope anymore and so have packed all my things into a hankie and am about to head out to the road to Londonium to see if I can hitch a lift.

The reason for my departure began last week.......

As I think I told you I upset Mum on my hack last week by bobbing off with her at mach 10, well ever since I swear she's just being trying to get back at me. On Sunday Mum decided that the sore patch behind my knee had got much worse and as I wouldn't let her look at it (its MY sore patch I can do what I like) she was going to call the vet.

Sure enough on Monday Herman the German vet came out with a new lady I'd not seen before. Mr German needle man listened to what Mum had to say about my leg and said to the lady "Dis horse vill let you do anysink to heem". On hearing this I had a sudden flash back to the invasion of my manly parts and decided that swiftly dispatching said vet via a quick kick to the head was the best course of action. In fairness it was only a warning shot but he moved out of the way pretty quick and decided to "sedate" me.

OMG. That sedation stuff is cool! My legs went all wobbly and I decided to have a lie down. This resulted in Mum squarking and trying to prop me up - a bit stupid when I'm a fair bit bigger than her. Anyway between her and Herman they kept me upright and I stood admiring the pretty coloured butterflies flying past inside my head and ignored what they were doing to me. BIG mistake. HUGE! When I finally came back down to earth they had PLUCKED me! I have a vast patch of feather missing..... I look like an owl with alopecia.....I have my very own crop circle behind my knees.....from the air if I lie down airplanes will think I have a landing strip up the back of my legs. My life is over. Added to which Mum has to put this horrible cream on my legs every day which I'm not too keen on. Look what happened last time she went near the back of my legs - the future of my feather depends on me keeping her OFF my legs. Admittedly she clings on pretty tight and does express herself so very fluently...

Anyway it doesn't appear to have put Dolly off but then that's because I cunningly only graze with my head towards her thus not letting her see the mass destruction behind my knees. She's getting quite smoochy and yesterday Mum was fuming when I refused to stop canoodling with Dolly and go to the gate. Huuummmm lets think why Mum - fit bird giving me a nuzzle behind my ears or my psychotic mother yielding a pot of cream and a pair of scissors. I know I am thick set but this doesn't mean I am thick.

Anyway Evil Army Man is coming later so that will just complete my week. How am I supposed to jump when mother has clipped off parts of my feathers? I am about to be beasted around the school when I should be in bereavement counselling for my bouffant. How can I, the Destroyer, both woo the ladies and wow the crowds when I look like I have mange?

So before he comes I am legging it - I would just hide in Dolly's rug bin but I tried fitting in there the other day and just because I can't see my Mum doesn't apparently mean she can't see me. Damn it.

So dear Diary I am left with no choice, to save my feathers, man hood and what's left of my reputation I am running away.

Now if someone could just give me directions from the wind turbine at the end of the road to London I'll be on my way....

05.11.2010

Dear Diary

As is evident by the fact I am able to write this I have quite clearly not run away. Finding a laptop under a hedge in Hackney may be difficult so I decided on reflection to stay put. That said it has been touch and go....

Last Friday afternoon HE came. Evil Army Man himself. I was already worried what horrors awaited when Mum volunteered us for a beasting with the words "we need someone to shout at us". WE? What's with the WE? I don't need anyone to shout at me - as for mother well whatever floats her boat....

Anyway what followed was a complete destruction of all the handy evasions I have been building up on Mum since we last saw EAM. It was all straightness, correct bend, correct strike off, no wiggling away from the fence, no squishing Mum legs into the fence (a particular fave of mine) and the reminding Mum of what that long thing she carries in her hand is for. Grrr! That man is SUCH a killjoy. He did finally let me do some jumping but only baby stuff as "we all know he can jump. Its how we get there that's important". Speak for yourself mate - its how I sail over them that gets me having any chance with the females of the species. He also muttered the immortal comment - "well its not as if he's a showjumper is it?". I am sorry!! I am not a what? How very dare you suggest that my manly figure is better used for pulling milk floats than it is for leaping forth over fences. I don't care how evil he is EAM is going to get to have a feather facial is he's not careful....

Anyway as usual when Mr Killjoy has been Mum then spent all weekend practising what he'd taught her. Boooorrriiiinnnnnngggg.

On Sunday night just as Mum was putting me in my PJs there was a commotion and a new lady walked into the barn. She's tall and ginger and from what I could see quite fit. As Mum had failed to secure my door correctly I thought I'd go and introduce myself. This didn't go down too well I have to say and I was swiftly banished back to my stable accompanied by several suggestions as to my parentage. Anyway I have not yet been able to make a move as she's at the other end of the stable block and not in field near me. My time will come however.

Yesterday Herman the German came back and shoved more needles in me and reported my legs are much improved. I tried once again to show him the new improved underside of my back feet but he didn't seem too keen to examine them.

This morning we have been out on our usual hack with Billy. It was a bit of a weird one as Billy came in from the field with his eyes all gummed up so I had to be his guide dawg. I managed to stand on my shoe within five minutes of leaving the yard so at least Billy had the sounds of me clinking to guide him. Mum didn't quite see this as a good thing so we only walked which is so beneath me these days. My athletic bouncing did nearly backfire after I fell up the verge and nearly landed on my nose. At this point I decided Mum had got the point and so I gave in to the walking idea. Then Aunty C dropped her whip and had to get off, which in essence was fine apart from the fact she couldn't get back on. So we had to try to find a hummock for her to stand on to remount. I was totally bemused by the whole experience by this point. Then after she had remounted in a herculean effort (come on woman Billy is NOT that big) we got halfway down the road and she dropped it again. Luckily there were two people walking by who clearly realised Mum and Aunty C were not safe to be allowed out on their own and picked up the whip for them. By this stage I had lost the will to live - being saddled with a plank for a mother is bad enough but when they start travelling in plank packs then I'm sorry but there should be a law against it. Anyway we survived, made it home and despite Mum blasting the backs of my knees with a hose pipe to rid my sore patches of the mud I had managed to plaster up my legs, I am in a good mood. Dolly is in the next field, mystery new bird in the field after that so I'm currently working on some manly moves up the fence line (stopping for food as necessary - and yes every 2 seconds is necessary) so I shall report back how successful I am next week.

I leave you with this thought - I am a big beefy Clyde, all manly and feathered - so why does everyone say I pee like a race horse? Should I be concerned?

19.11.2010

Dear Diary
I think I may possibly be spending the foreseeable future incommunicado sharing my meagre rations with the thing that barks. It'll be lonely this Christmas, lonely and blue, it'll be lonely this Christmas living with doogiedoo……….. what do you think? Christmas number 1?

Anyway firstly apologies for not writing last week – Mum had the affront to work last Friday and as usual took the laptop with her. I have suggested she needs to buy me my own but after this weeks antics I think I have about as much hope as a carrot has of surviving within my reach……

It was Mum and I's anniversary at the weekend – 3 years since I arrived and chose her as my human. As a result she came home on the Saturday and gave me a big hug.

Followed by a big squark when she caught sight of the very large love bite Dolly had given me the day before. Now I must admit I'm all for some hot and heavy foreplay but I did worry the girl was going for my jugular, I'd not thought to check her teeth for length so suddenly started realising I'd never seen her eat garlic.... Yikes!!

It was a very big bite and Mum was NOT happy – I heard her having words with Dolly later on so that's ruined any chance I might have had. My mothers "little words" are legendary........

Anyway Mum bought me a nice big molasses lick for an anniversary present. I'd not got her anything so swiftly spat my dinner at her for her gift. From her reaction she was over the moon with my present; her voice got all excited and she jumped for joy.

Now at this junction I have to point out that Mum knows I usually make a mess with my licks. This is not a new thing and I can't help it. I have to use my face to prop up the licky thing when it gets all slippery and wet so there's little wonder I have it all over my face......and down my legs........ooops. Even I don't know how I got it in my ears but heh I am a talented boy and who knows what I get up to in my sleep? This led to a very embarrassing hour long scrub on Tuesday night to rid my face of lickit before I saw Cool New Shoes Man on weds. Mum however forgot to remove the licky thing overnight so she was thrilled to bits to see me back in the same state on weds morning. I am sure she uses the word "tramp" as a sign of affection – she says it so often it can't be anything but that.

On Monday and Tuesday morning I was impressing the barn by demonstrating my amazing throwing powers. Mum helpfully leaves all sorts of things for me to throw about – usually towels and head collars and things, but this week the stick thing with the string that makes me go to sleep was also there so I has great fun wanging that about as well. Unfortunately I was going for a record in the feed bucket fling when boss lady Sarah walked by. Does she not know not to venture into a live wanging zone? Thankfully the feed bucket did miss her, but not by much.........

Apparently my behaviour and that of my retired older brother this week has driven mother to the brink. The brink of where? And how is this my fault? I don't even have a driving licence – I'm too young I think.

Wednesday night when Cool New Shoes Man came she tied me up outside my stable as it was dark outside and he needed the light – why I'm not sure as I'm pretty sure my feet are where they've always been but heh if that's what the man needs. I got a little bored waiting for him to finish so decided to help out by rubbing all the writing off the white board on the wall. How was I supposed to know you use a cloth? Oh and that green and blue marker pen shows up really well on white noses? Sheesh the fuss that was made! Mother was making funny moaning noises and rocking slightly but I'm sure that was due to the cold....

Yesterday a new lady, funky back lady, came to see me. She was very small and wore a funky coloured hat and cool boots with shoelaces I kept undoing. She thought that was funny and "very cute" – why can't my mother think like that? She wriggled me about all over the place and did insist on trying to wrap my legs around my head. I'm flexible lovey but not that flexible. Apparently I have hurt my poll which is why I have been leaning on Mums hands. HA!!! I have been vindicated. I demanded mother take back all the nasty things she's said about my parentage of late; admittedly I did demand a little too hard and Mum ended up face first in a haynet but heh I think she got my point!

Anyway funky back lady did all sorts of weird things to me and said I should be fine. But apparently my right bum is not as muscled as my left bum. She said all posh words about it but I can confirm that it was my bum she was poking. Now Mum has been given carte blanche to pull my tail every day. I fail to see how this is fair so I pulled a chunk of Mums hair in return. I didn't mean for it to come out in my mouth though....semi bald is not a look Mum is carrying off very well I have to add.

So what with the accidental scalping, the molasses, the joy ride I give her on my legs every time she puts cream on the back of my knees and the antics bringing me in at night now its dark (I'm not scared of the dark – that would be unmanly- but I do think we should walk quicker than we do when its light) I think Mum is looking back lovingly over our last 3 years together. I'm sure that's what she meant when she said she was reflecting on her options? One of these options apparently means we might be going to a BBQ soon which will be nice, although Diary what large prat burgers are I have no idea?????

26.11.2010

Dear Diary

I am now a grown up big boy. I know this because my Mum has told me so this morning, just before she wacked me on the bum with a whip and told me I therefore had to man up and stop being a Poof about the wheelie bin. Now I must point out it was a GREY wheelie bin and this was the issue. Wheelie bins should be green, black or brown not GREY. Now I am not stupid so thus I had already realised this was a horse eating monsters cunning disguise and was trying to save us both. Alas once again my mother proved Darwin might have had a point and insisted on dying at the hands of the wheelie bin morphed monster. Admittedly we didn't actually die but we MIGHT have, so I feel vindicated.

Furthermore last weekend Mum and Dad have decided as I am now a big grown up boy to put me back into my snaffle in the school. This followed me annoying the bum off mother on Saturday and only having two speeds - Stop and Go. Having threatened me with all sorts of dire consequences if I didn't start behaving she wheeled out the big guns on Sunday. i.e. Dad. So just to annoy her I behaved like an angel for Dad, all light and floaty, prancing about like a big dressage princess. Now I know when Mums REALLY peed off because she goes all sulky, every second word is "FINE" in that tone that indicates in fact its not at all, and she sighs a lot. So me doing a perfect leg yield all the way down the school in a snaffle for Dad was indeed "FINE", followed by more sighing than I do when forced to listen to EAMs lectures on "softness". In fairness she got on and I behaved for her too just in case Dad wasn't doing my tea that night - heh I may be big but don't think I'm dumb!

In the meantime Dolly has not forgiven me for mother having a little "word" with her the other week about her giving me a love bite. In fact I think mother may have forced her to bat for the other side. She's spending more time smooching the ginger mare than me and whilst I might like watching for a while it bothers me that I am giving off all the wrong signals. First of all I make Stallions get all frisky and now I'm turning women into lady lovers. Do people really think I'm camper than Alan Carr in a tent? Sheesh what do I have to do to convince these ladies that I am 100% all Irish bog trotting beef cake? Admittedly with hindsight wetting myself in the dark on the lunge last night right in front of the ladies probably didn't help my cause but how was I supposed to know the big bogey man at B was actually Bernie the bouncing bunny? It was dark, he was in shadow, and it was an easy mistake to make......... Mum is still moaning about her shoulder this morning but it was her daft idea to hang on whilst I launched myself into outer space so I fail to see this is my fault.

I am now enjoying the sunshine, the view of two lovely ladies playing tongue bits and chomping on my grass. I shall await my daily tail pulling and carrot teasing when mother gets back. I tell you I can't ruddy wait..........

03.12.2010

Dear Diary
Its official.
My mother has lost the plot.
Completely and totally lost it.

Last year when the white stuff came it was apparent that it killed horses. For this reason we were all kept inside safe and sound until the white stuff gave up lying in wait and left. All good sensible stuff, carried out by my sensible Mum and sensible Aunties.

This year I think Mum has had too many blows to the head. She made me GO OUTSIDE in the middle of the advance of the enemy white stuff. It sneakily tried to blind me by flying in my eyes, deafen me by blowing in my ears, crippled me by holding on to my feet, starve me by hiding all the grass and my mother LEFT me in it! The other day we stayed in for a few hours then Mum took me in the ménage and tried to make me run with her in it. Do I look retarded? It was bad enough Mum was leaping about in the snow looking like she was out on day release without expecting me to do the same. Prancing about like a great lemon Poof in the white stuff may make for "lovely pictures" but they do little for a boys street cred.... Yesterday the white stuff had laid such siege to the drive I was sure that we would all stay in safe and warm but no! Boss lady Sarah took down some of the fencing so we could walk around the long way - and boy was it a llooooooonnnngggg way - to our fields. What is with these people?

We walked out to the fields in twos (I went with Dolly which was the only good thing as I got to oggle her butt from 6 inches) and we were nearly dead by the time we got there. The snow was up to my knees, past my Mums knees, very deep and very cold! Mum was sounding like she was making a dirty phone call by the time we got halfway round and I seriously could not think of a single thing that could have been waiting for me in that field that would have made that trip worth it. Well other than my lovely and much missed fit mare. Covered in molasses. Holding a bag of carrots. Huummm. Excuse me while I wipe off the drool from the side of my mouth, its not a good look and knowing my luck will freeze my face to the stable door. I do not want to spend the day looking like a stuck on Garfield.

By the time we got to the field I'd probably lost more calories than I was going to eat that day - it was like the outdoor pursuit equivalent of celery - more effort than its worth. I had cold feathers, 6 inch stilettos, a runny nose and a serious aversion to that white stuff. Then I see all that slog was for a hay nets worth of hay spread out on the snow. WTF?!

136

I nearly DIED and all I get is HAY? The very least I was expecting was carrots, a cup of that stuff Mum drinks and an hour with Dolls. Hubba hubba, I'd warm her up! By breathing heavily on her obviously - I was far too pooped for anything more than that Then blow me to come in in the afternoon we had to repeat the entire performance. Hah! Not likely! I came in like an exocet on speed. Well tried to. The combination of Dad on the end of the rope, the white stuff launching a sustained attack on visibility, a badly timed spook and a large snow drift put pay to that idea........ If anyone asks I was making a horse angel alright?

Today is not much better although because it is very icy Mum has said I'm not going out until mid morning. I'm planning on burying so far under my bed that she can't see me in the vain hope of not having to do the snow marathon again. I'm hoping that by breathing in I can disguise myself as a bank?

Failing that has anyone got room in a suitcase that's travelling somewhere hot?

10.12.2010

Dear Diary
I think my chances of getting a nice Christmas present have this week gone from slim to positively anorexic.

Some of this I do take the blame for but not all: It is not my fault that we have more snow here than Siberia or that the temperatures have only made polar bears happy. It is therefore not my fault that the fields and the paths to the fields are frozen solid. It may possibly be my fault that I have found it most amusing to nudge Mum in the back just before the slight slope down to my field. Eddie the Eagle would be proud of some of the take offs she's made...

It is also not entirely my fault that I am a big boy and thus find walking on the 3 inch strip of grit that Boss lady Sarah has put down rather difficult. Besides which ice skating is great fun even if I have been told I resemble Scooby Doo on speed. I assume this is not a compliment? The fact that if I slip I make Mum slip is a minor point - she has a large bum and so is well cushioned. If she full on kissed concrete I would feel bad but merely bouncing on her bum is hardly an issue, not that this is something we're seeing eye to eye on; mainly because I'm 16.2HH and she's on the floor...........

But my complete fall from grace came on Wednesday night. Dolly had gone in first and had shook her bum at me on the way past in a way that makes Beyonce look like an amateur. So when she started calling for me from within the stable I was so excited I pranced for joy. Unfortunately Ronnie must have thought she was yelling to him because he started rearing like a stallion. Now the fact his Mum was on the end of the lead rope at the time was unfortunate but heh hum. Now I was NOT having that prancing princess nicking my girl so I thought it was high time I showed him some Destroyer moves. Now in hindsight doing this on a frozen field whilst Mum was trying to catch me might not go down as the greatest move on my part but I'm a young boy and my hormones just took over. After 10 minutes I'm sure he'd got the point and the fit ginger mare had definitely seen me in a new light so I allowed mother to catch me. I once again marvel at my mothers grasp of the English language and the fact when she's on one she doesn't seem to pause for breath. Since then I understand she has offered me free to a good home so I think maybe, just maybe, she was not impressed?

Anyway in the midst of all my cavorting I managed to pull a shoe off (double ooops) so today replacement shoe man came (Cool New Shoes Man is away apparently). He said how mannerly and lovely I am - Mum must have agreed because she snorted so hard she made a snot bubble. She is such an embarrassment. I have been creeping like mad since Wednesday day, nuzzling her, cuddling her and generally kissing bum in a hope that she won't carry out her promise to tether me to the side of the road and leave.

That said I'm not happy with her anyway. Apparently she posted some silly letter on Horse and Hound online forum and it got published on their face book page. I have no idea what that is but how come I don't make it there? Mum says people think she's funnier than me. Funnier than me? Never.

What goes 99, bonk, 99, bonk?
A caterpillar with a wooden leg

What's brown and sticky?
A stick

Why did the pony go to the vets?
Because he was a little hoarse

Badda bish!
Thank you!!

I am available for weddings, christenings and hay baling parties (well providing Mum hasn't sold me into slavery in Siberia).

So me, all 4 shoes, my hay and this infernal ice are hanging out in the field. I am hoping Mum attempts to poo pick again today - watching her prising frozen poo off the grass is hilarious. Especially when the fork suddenly springs out of the ground showering her in frozen poo pellets...... Note to self try to snigger subtly - Siberia is cold at this time of year............

The letter
Diary in case any of you are interested this is the stupid letter Mum wrote that got published. I don't think its even faintly amusing.........

Letter to the man upstairs

Dear Man Upstairs
First of all I would like to thank you for the first lot of snow: it was pretty for a while, kind of nice to have some snow at Christmas time, allowed me to take some nice pictures of Hovis in the snow etc etc.

But if I may now point out enough is enough, time to move on.

My reasons for this request are simple and are as follows:

1. Whilst I have a very well padded behind I feel no need to keep testing my arse airbags by falling on it repeatedly. Once was amusing. After the 10th time I now have a backside that resembles a rotten potato.

2. Hovis is not Bambi. Whilst Bambi on ice is cute, 3/4 of a tonne of flayling Destroyer is less so. I accept it may be my fault that my steed has no sense of self preservation but if you could just cut me a little slack that would be great.

3. Whilst I know I may resemble a Russian shot putter I feel no need to have to keep competing in the ice trough discus. Just one day of not having to wrestle a 4 inch thick Frisbee of ice out of a trough would be lovely.

4. If I had wanted to be a builder I would have become one. I am ill equipped to use hammers and blow torches to get water pipes unfrozen. I thank you for the opportunity to learn new skills but I am dangerous and quite frankly should stick to what I know best.

5. I know I am unfit. There is no need to repeatedly keep proving this by forcing me to wade 3/4 of a mile through thigh deep snow. Whilst seeing me panting harder than that weird man who keeps ringing my mobile number might seem amusing I'm not seeing the funny side.

6. Snot icicles are only funny when you are 5. As I am now 33 I feel that this is not a look I need to sport. Furthermore the only thing that a red nose looks cute on is Rudolph.

7. If I wanted to feed my horse hay popsicles I'd make him some. Please do not feel the need to assist me any further in my horses nutritional needs.
8. Finally -16 is the number of dresses sizes I'd like to drop, not my idea of a desirable temperature.

In summary whilst I am very grateful for the opportunity of taking lots of lovely photos, thus providing me with some very cheap Christmas cards, I would now like to request a return to normal temperatures. I promise hand on heart not to complain about mud, dirty rugs, wet feet or mucky feathers. At least for a week or so.............

Yours Sincerely

Slowly defrosting of Lincolnshire

17.12.2010

Dear Diary
I would like to send the man upstairs a Christmas card. Does anyone know his address? I want to thank him for the three week holiday from riding I have had and suggest he keeps the good work up - retirement is FUN!!

I was a little concerned when the white stuff started to melt but the sheet ice, frozen ménage and driving sleet are inspired! That said if he could turn the radiator up a little bit that would be great. This morning I am mostly wearing a cardboard rug. Whilst it is dry it is also frozen - I look like Hovis-in-a-box. Between wetting herself with laughing mother has attempted to mould it to my manly frame but on last inspection my tail flap is sticking up at a particularly jaunty angle. This I feel sends out the wrong signals to my ladies so I'm hoping I have a hot ass to melt it swiftly and return it to its normal position. If it stays sticking up much longer I'm going to become the next stopping place for migrating lesser spotted bird things.

In other weather related news my coaching for Mums attempt to appear on prancing on ice has gained momentum. We have now mastered the downhill flail to the field and are now working on the 360-piroutte-whilst-trying-to-undo-the gate-tapes. Yesterdays attempt was almost worthy of a 6 if she hadn't slipped, grabbed for me, missed and almost head butted the fence post. Admittedly "missed" tends to infer it was her fault and lack of aim rather than my very subtle sidestep out of reach but heh as she says to me - you learn by your mistakes.

Mum and I also have a very cool new game. She lets me off at the gate, puts the tape up and I rush off to see Dolly, prancing (in a manly fashion) and showing off my moves. I then come back to assist Mum defrost my ice trough (in my opinion I do a better job but she seems to get a little upset when I stamp my foot in the bucket at the same time as she does) and then we run. Mum runs to the end of the field and I run alongside till we get to the electric fence. Then Mum moves it back the whopping 6 inches that she allows me, she goes home and I eat. All great fun and rather majestic looking. Yesterday however our game went a little wrong. For once I was behind Mum rather than at the side and I had a little bit of brake failure. I think its fair to say we have discovered the stopping distance for a Destroyer on ice is a fair distance.......... I crashed into Mum causing her to make a lightening quick decision. Attempt to stop or jump the electric fence. Mum has a lot of bone and the aerodynamic properties of an elephant with concrete wellies on, so she elected for attempting to stop. Ooopps. The good news is I didn't get bitten by the fence.... bad news is mother did. To be honest the fuss she made you'd think it hurt or something, admittedly I perhaps should have given her a cuddle or something before turning round and eating grass..... and allowing my natural gases to escape in her direction. Last seen she was muttering darkly about sale rooms, glue and taking up knitting. I think the electric might have caused a momentary brain fart? I hope.........

I also need to get word to my retired older brother. It appears his selflessness saved me from a "hot ragging" the other day. Mum had gone to see him, groomed him, hot ragged him and generally tried to make him look presentable. I was apparently the next stop on her hot ragging rampage. Thankfully Sids timely spitting of a half a bucket of cold water down my mothers neck so demoralised her that I was saved. He may have used to kick my butt from one end of the field to the other but I owe him one. I did think of sending him half of my swede but decided I wasn't THAT grateful.

Besides I have other worries. Its kissmuss soon - usually a time I look forward to for much snogging under the hay nets with fit furry lovelies. But Diary I am in a male dominated yard now - how does that work? Billy's a total dude but he eats a LOT of garlic and has a moustache.. Can I please cancel kissmuss this year?

24.12.2010

Dear Diary
Happy Kissmuss!
Apologies for the tardiness of my entry today but we have been having technical issues. Well more like mother issues to be honest. She's in Spain seeing my Grandma and Granddad so I have had to dictate my entry over the phone to her for her to write it down. This is due to her ongoing refusal to buy me my own laptop and led to major issues with her forgetting her log on details. This does not surprise me one little bit as every day she seems to forget I am a big boy and insists on calling me all sorts of embarrassing names in front of the ladies.

Anyway this week has seen me still retired. I am LOVING it! The journey to the fields is fun as I get to see Mum slithering all over and expressing herself with positively amazing fluency. Who needs that Torvil and Dean pair? I've got mother doing Bolero with a fence post and a yard of electrical fencing.... Plus watching her puffing along bringing my water and hay is priceless. Bambi on ice has nothing on Mum and a large water carrier.

I continue to help Mum break the ice out of my bucket and carry my haynet up the field which I know she secretly loves.... well I'm sure that's what she means really when she suggests I might be retarded?

Earlier this week my next door neighbour Barney was taken ill. He had a bad tummy ache and boss lady Sarah came out at all hours to give him some really yummy stuff called peppermint tea to drink. I know its yummy because I feigned dehydration and she let me have some too. She put extra sugar in mine which was brave - I'm not sure she's seen what sugar does to a Destroyer yet.... I'm also not sure Mum is getting the idea that this is how I should be treated so I'm working on educating her. Boss lady Sarah's foal likes me and I have now trained him to bring me carrots and apples. The fact he fed me all the family's vegetables that were meant for their tea the other day did not go down well but I was well happy. Mother was rather embarrassed but heh if my fans wish to feed me what can I do?

So Mum is away for Kissmuss which means I get a quiet one with the lads and lots of presents when she gets back. Plus hopefully some under the haynet action with Dolly later tonight. At least I hope so - we're drawing straws to see who gets to snog who. I've bribed little Arnie to tell me which one is the longest straw as he's so small he can see underneath. I'm not spending kissmuss playing tonsil tennis with Tom, no way José!

But despite all the fun of kissmuss I am also sad today as it was a year ago I lost the one true love of my life - fit mare.

142

I've written a little poem for her:

Its been a year since I lost my girl
An awful day that changed my world
Every day I miss her still
And forever more I always will
I can close my eyes and see her there
My black beauty, my fit mare
Coat like satin, dark as night
Four little socks shining white

She's at my shoulder running free
Wherever I am, she comes with me
Because she's in my heart, in my soul
Forever young, never growing old

She's over the bridge, on the other side
With all the horses who've ever died
Waiting for us all to meet again
When our lives have come to journeys end

In loving memory of Minnie "Moo" Marshall.
I miss you gorgeous girl

31.12.2010

Dear Diary

Happy New Years Eve! I know its New Years Eve because Mum is claiming to start her diet tomorrow and we're organising a party for tonight. Bring on the midnight snog fest – only with the ladies I hasten to add – I'm not being funny but I don't wish to get my moustache locked with Billy's in time for the New Year.......

I am however a little concerned about this New Year as Mum has told me I have to think of some New Year revolutions. I didn't know what revolution meant so I asked old Tom who said it meant an uprising. Billy said it meant going round in circles so I am confused: maybe they are both right and I have to rise up and spin round all at the same time? This deeply concerns me as I'm pretty sure that rearing and spinning were what got Fancy pants ejected from the building – besides which such a feat requires a level of limb co-ordination that I'm not sure I have? Do you think Mum will settle for me doing a fairly nifty turn on the forehand instead?

Anyway that is a problem for tomorrow. Today's problem is how to engineer the snogging so I get to play tongue bits with Dolly or the aloof ginger one at midnight and not Billy, Barney or Tom et al. I'm all for bromance but not playing tonsil hockey with a dude nearly as big as me who eats a LOT of garlic. I'm also concerned that we may end up listening to old tunes on the radio and reminiscing about the time "in 1900 and wash your socks" rather than getting down to some banging tunes and drinking peppermint tea. There is a serious age gap between me and my house mates and sometimes I do feel like they're more pipe, slippers and tweed saddle cloths whereas I am more of an R&B loving, fur saddle cloth sporting dude. Ah well we shall have to see.

So it's farewell to this year, hello next year.

This year has seen me gain a brother, move house, lose a brother, have my retired brother move closer to home, do lots of jumping (yippee!), do even more poncing (boo hiss) and finally after 3 years finally go stubble racing with Mum! I have had my first summer romance, learnt that fences can bite, finally moved on from my beloved fit mare and made some cool new friends.

Like my lickits I can't believe how quickly this year has gone but just like those lovely sugary treats (just in case Mum is reading this) I can't wait for the next one!

So I'll see you in 2011 Diary.

Until then, goodbye 2010, this is the Destroyer. Out.

Contact details

Bransby Horses
Address: Bransby,
           Lincoln,
           LN1 2PH

Web: www.bransbyhorses.co.uk
Tel: 01427 788464
Email: mail@bransbyhorses.co.uk

Pilar Larcade, Artist
Web: http://pilar-larcade.110mb.com
or   Facebook: Pilar Larcade, Artist.

Karen Thompson and Hovis, Author(s)!
Mail: c/o Bransby Horses
           Bransby,
           Lincoln,
           LN1 2PH